BODY DROP

BODY
DROP

*Notes on Fandom
and Pain in
Professional Wrestling*

BRIAN OLIU

THE UNIVERSITY OF NORTH CAROLINA PRESS

Chapel Hill

Designed and set by Jamison Cockerham in Scala and Bleecker.

Cover photograph by Patrick Case, courtesy of Pexels.com.

The University of North Carolina Press has been a
member of the Green Press Initiative since 2003.

Manufactured in the United States of America

LIBRARY OF CONGRESS CATALOGING-IN-PUBLICATION DATA
Names: Oliu, Brian, author.
Title: Body drop : notes on fandom and pain in
    professional wrestling / Brian Oliu.
Description: Chapel Hill : The University of North Carolina Press, [2021]
Identifiers: LCCN 2021000644 | ISBN 9781469663401 (cloth)
    | ISBN 9781469663418 (paperback) | ISBN 9781469663425 (ebook)
Subjects: LCSH: Wrestling—Social aspects—United States.
    | Wrestling—United States. | Wrestlers—United States.
    | LCGFT: Essays.
Classification: LCC GV1196.4.S63 O55 2021 | DDC 796.8120973—dc23
LC record available at https://lccn.loc.gov/2021000644

For CAMELLIA *and* JASON,

always ready for the hot tag—houses of fire, both

You bastards just count little scores,
but I'm not like that. I'm risking my life.

MINORU SUZUKI

What happens next depends on what you believe and
why, what you're given and the proof you require.

COLETTE ARRAND

I'm not the shark. I'm not a fish.
I'm not an avalanche. I'm a man.

JOHN TENTA

CONTENTS

PART TWO *Listen to This Crowd*
....

PART THREE *Surely This Is It*

BODY
DROP

PART ONE

INTRODUCING FIRST

Tie-Up

There are many secrets to wrestling, and this is the first: it is only 25 percent fake. The rest is as real as you, or me, or the memories that we hold. That is to say, we ache in ways that radiate from places that we cannot pinpoint. There is truth here, if we can only find the source.

Mark Henry, the World's Strongest Man, Is the World's Strongest Man

And he is a rarity in this world, where we use hyperbole to mean something truer than fact: showstopper, human wrecking ball, the most beautiful woman in our world. He is stronger than the two of us put together, I promise you that, as my arms are not as large as his and yours are smaller than mine, delicate in their existence. When we imagine the world's strongest man, what do we imagine? Someone with shoulders that block out the sun, the strength to uproot every tree, the ability to push a trailer with one hand—a comic book character with a square jaw and a bright smile, chiseled from white marble, an Atlas that has climbed to the other side of the world and left it spinning on its axis. Instead, he is someone who would never be drawn: dark skin, rough beard, as heavy as the weight he can lift.

I think of him as a child as I think of myself as a child: thick waist, double chin. My mother would drive me to the gym and leave me there among iron. I would walk between the machines with names I could never pronounce; I would look at drawings of sinews and bone disbelieving that those red muscles pulled taut existed in me somewhere underneath all that I am. I could do all of this if I had the right shoes. I could do all of this if I were prepared: shorts longer, wrists taped, fingers interwoven and pressed out in front of my chest as a signal that it is time to get to work. Instead, I would walk, eyes on the conveyor below, my neck pulling toward the ground as I watched shoelace flop over leather, lamenting the fact that this is all wrong: that to be the world's strongest man is to not only know what strength is but to know what the world holds.

When the world's strongest man bleeds, it is red. His heart does not pump sugar water, his blood is not thinner than any of ours. The world's strongest man picks up a person you love into the air: he places his hands underneath their arms and pushes the person you love toward the sky until they are resting on his shoulder, his beard brushing against the side of their stomach. He asks you what this person does, and before you start to tell him about the beauty of it all, the blue nights, the hands in hands, the world's strongest man, chalk underneath his fingernails, loses his grip. This person you love falls to the floor. You do not have the heart to tell him that this person does not do anything now; you do not have the heart to tell him any of these things—that the world's strongest man reads things backward, that he has lost a child, that loving him is a joke that weaker men play on him, that he is not what we pictured him to be, that he cannot be run through. You do not tell him any of this because he is the world's strongest man, and this is what he knows to be true: that 800 pounds is 800 pounds, that the iron does not lie, that you can lift something or you cannot.

After the world's strongest man dies, I will be the world's strongest man. When I am the world's strongest man, I will tell the world this story: When I was a child, we were the same. I would stop walking. I would sit and watch the television screens: here is someone not as strong as the world's strongest man being praised for his strength, here is a woman on trial. I would dunk my head underwater like in a baptism, like I had just won all of the things that the world wished to offer me—I would wipe the water on my shirt. I will hold my breath; I will be red in the face. I have worked hard for this. I am wearing the wrong shoes. You will laugh and I will laugh because what a beautiful story that is: that the truth here is simple: there is nothing here besides the willingness to grasp what is perceived as impossible to hold.

LET ME TELL YOU SOMETHING

It starts in Gorilla—production setting up behind
the final curtain, producers with headphones
relaying messages to the announcer's table,
television cameras showing every broadcast angle.
The area is named after the late announcer Gorilla
Monsoon, who would interview wrestlers right
before their march down to the ring—the last
possible moment anyone can be themselves.

Back-Body Drop

The secret is wrestlers are never ready.

Despite them taking bumps over and over again, there is always a moment of bracing. There are hours of practice—of diagraming an entire match that ends with a huge spot, a moment when a wrestler goes crashing through a table or a powerbomb being taken on the side of the ring apron.

My body is never ready for anything that I throw at it. It is difficult to assume that my body is not ready, because this would mean that I know my body—how it operates under these circumstances, how despite never running for more than a handful of minutes at a time, it can somehow understand the task ahead of me and know exactly where it should be, what it should look like. I am far from optimized, and I am aware of this: that there could be a beautiful moment where existing in the world is simply a task that needs to be done and nothing more—that I am literally going through the motions.

Days before my first marathon, my right leg locks up. It is a run like any other run—a celebration of the end of marathon training, of surviving something that seemed impossible months ago. The race has always been less about the race and more about what needed to be done for the race—the day of is supposed to be a coronation, a day where everything goes beautifully, a day where I can stop at water stations every couple of miles, rather than forcing myself to go hours without drinking, occasionally hiding a plastic bottle in the bushes for the second loop, all the while hoping that a stray dog doesn't puncture the plastic with its teeth. The day of coronation before the coronation ends with my leg refusing to straighten—the knee permanently fixed in a half bend, as if I were the perfect model for a caricature of a person running: leg lifted in the air while the arms punch skyward. I, too, am like the drawing, frozen in motion, waiting for the other shoe to drop.

I would like to tell you that this was sudden: when you hear stories of injuries, you can pinpoint the exact moment of disaster. There was no pop, no grand flailing about—instead, silence, as if nothing about this was anything but routine. There is no moment when the foot strike reverberates up and through the leg, sending a bludgeoning shock through the body. There is glory in failure—a grand gesture of the body breaking: a torn tendon coiling down the back of a leg and resting in a spiraled heap at the bottom of a calf, a bone splintering and piercing through what was otherwise flat. Instead, at one moment, I could run, and the next moment I could not.

Wrestlers never know which routine bump is going to be their last. Tyson Kidd was nearly paralyzed after a Muscle Buster—a move he has taken 100 times or more, where all of the impact is absorbed in the back, but it was his spinal cord that declared it had had too much. Paige's career ended on a kick to the back, her head whipping backward as if she were in a car wreck, before flopping to the canvas, unable to feel her arms or feet.

Wrestling is a career notorious for hanging on too long. There are stories of '80s stars taking punishment in VFW halls, selling high-gloss Polaroids of themselves in their prime out of the backs of their rental cars. The greatest achievement is to go out on one's own terms: to decide exactly when and where to retire. It is customary for veterans to go out on their backs—they lose their final rivalries to someone younger in an attempt to put them over with the crowd, as this is a true finale, a standing ovation after a passing of the torch. It doesn't seem like too much to ask—and yet a sword is a sword, whether it is being laid down or cutting us down at the knees.

Triple H and Why There Are
Fights in Locker Rooms

To be the king of kings means that we must know what royalty is: the ability to govern without the knowledge of a kingdom—no interest in lakes and mud but only crowns, the way we imagine these old men in their furs and lavender, beards down to their bellies. The blood, blue as calm, remains the same as it always has been, asking a question on the ocean as if there is something else there, something new in its entirety. This is an ode to joy, as if joy has left us entirely and we are left with a machine that knows nothing of quaintness— the only thing left to do is be the largest person in the room: these attempts at immortality, this need to be thought of as something that remains connected to the universe long after the divine fades away.

To rule those that rule there must be something here and intact: not like an egg, or a torn tendon that snapped and spun up your leg like a faulty window blind, but something deliberate: hard as a hammer, swung with the force of someone testing their strength, trying to win at a game that simply counts up from rest, a small plunger striking a bell to let the world know of the conquest, that if you hear the ringing you are mine now, to hold or to not hold, to crush or to let sleep flat against the wall like a moth in a house with no lamps.

I did not envy you and your position: the governing with a coldness, the pointing from behind turrets, the hull down in the dead ground. My family, they are farmers, and their families, farmers as well, arms full of eggplants as violet as harmony—the idea that we can be seen from anywhere, that the fields have not frosted over despite it being many degrees colder here than in the city. I will say, I miss the city: its bulbous colors, its troubled marks, the falling asleep on couches before the stories end, the hopes of dinging out in the morning. Here, we need things to break concrete—there are no clippers to cut the grass, there are no ways in or out that don't involve growth: things living, even the skulls of dried-out animals seem alive in the tall ferns. Instead, we have steel on brick, steel to our guts—destruction work, the name meaning to strike, violently and cleanly, all things rigid. You never swing for the fences; you swing like a man who has never worked a day in his life, you swing like a king untested: you keep your sword sheathed at your side—it slaps against your thigh, against your jacket made from leather of a cow that someone else slaughtered.

And you represent us, somehow: the voice of a generation. The contrast between anarchy and monarchy is as thin as mists of water spat into the air; it is possible to hold the nozzle down on the spray can until the paint builds and thickens, layers to something solid: a throne to sit upon. We join you: your salute the same as ours, an insult to our enemies, an insult with so much boyishness that it seems silly now—something we do ironically because we know better, a game, of course, of who can run the fastest, who can shut the mouth of the meekest, who will have all the points at the end of something with uncertain rules. We play in locker rooms, harbingers of sweat and fungus, where even the soap we use to wash our bodies is rough to the touch, would peel layers away if your skin was soft, all perceived weaknesses removed, all things turned to stone and sledge. We are ourselves and we are you. We are mountains. We are royal. We are so far from man.

LET ME TELL YOU SOMETHING

Every wrestler has entrance music—you can often
tell how much stake the company has in a performer
by the quality of their introduction. The good
themes start with an interruption—a single note
that rings out to let the world know that business
is about to pick up. Stone Cold's glass break. Ric
Flair's signature "Woooo!" before the build of *Also
sprach Zarathustra.* The Rock's "If You Smell What
the Rock Is Cooking," complete with drum breaks
in between the pauses. Someone is always waiting
around to be interrupted.

Wristlock

The secret is the simplest things are the most difficult.

I was pulled into this world by my wrist—my body in my mother's womb twisted upward and around, to the point where the umbilical cord wrapped around my neck. A quick yank and I was free: alive, and nerves shredded like a shoelace that had begun to unravel after one day untied on the playground.

On that same playground, my arm does not swing correctly. Instead of swinging out in front of me, it drops to its side—sometimes finding its way across my body, constantly pulling my hips and legs to the left. I pull my body in one direction constantly, to the point where I cannot balance: up on one foot before I topple over. No skateboards, no bicycles.

For most of my life, I never gave it much thought. Instead, I kept my hand tucked away in a front pocket, walking in a rush, shoulders dipping forward. When I lift a drink to my lips, my elbow juts outward instead of up, parallel to the horizon. I was always asked why I drank so strangely, why I needed to take up even more space than my body granted me. It was a complicated answer: you'd need to understand the word "brachial," you'd need to know what a plexus is, you'd need to understand that birth is complicated, that we are delivered into this world.

Instead of answering, I would reach my hands out in front of me: my left palm pointed to the sky, my right palm open but unmoving, ready to receive a glass of water rather than a blessing. I'd show the lack of rotation: explain the word "supination" even though I did not yet know the word—I simply knew "stuck," or you might say "broken" or "freakish."

In mixed martial arts, wristlocks are considered to be impractical—an early and simple move learned in judo and jiujitsu that anyone who has some background in martial arts could easily defend against: a quick elbow strike with the other hand, your opponent's hands occupied while you can land a left fist flush anywhere you want.

In wrestling, wristlocks are an illusion: they are seen to be transitional moves that always lead to something larger and greater. You lock the wrist. You manipulate the fingers for effect. Your opponent swings wildly to break the hold before hitting the ropes hard. They charge at you with all they've got.

I would invite anyone to grab my wrist and force my palm upward, knowing that the second they let go, it would snap quickly back into place rather than staying where it was forced. It was a grand trick, and soon every dust-shoed boy was lining up to see if he could be the one to make it stick, using more and more force, wrenching my arm as if causing more pain is the best way to undo trauma, something they undoubtedly believe to be true. It doesn't hurt, I would say, although I knew that was an invitation to try harder to cause me to wince—if they couldn't win one game, they could win another.

Heartbreak; or, How I Felt When Shawn Michaels Threw His Best Friend through a Window

The story of heartbreak does not start here, but it could: a smile from a man who lost his face and gained a sense of faith in breaking the occipital bone instead of lowering the ears, feet skipping off the water and into cartilage: 100 plates rumored, a good round number in a world of hyperbole, but you could touch the screws if you wanted to, the zygomatic shimmering like elephants' armor, like a barber's clippers. The story of heartbreak is an odd one, as it always starts with the other: with midnights dropped from monikers because there should be no darkness here—all the world neon, all the world hot pink and mantis-colored and loud. Here are the accidents, in order: fingers in chests, bravado, the third to last bourbon, the last night of what we are left with—and what we are left with is this: a false embrace and a broken window—the other, heartbroken, the other, down window, while heartbreak is decreed baron of highfall, of leather, of sweat and smirk.

We should have known: there are no treaties here in this universe—everything is intentional. When feelings go sour there is no stopping the tartness: the acid building up on tongues and in our blood, which trickles from our foreheads in a jagged pattern, the result of false glass and real sharpness; heartbreak has no time for weakness, for closed fists in parking lots instead of open fists in the open. When your arm gets raised, you are champion, you are joy, yet you are seconds away from a forearm to the neck—something you've felt before: someone's skin under your chin for a brief moment, something to dust off, something to scramble up from like you've been startled awake and need to move in something other than circles. Something like that, yes. Some things shock, and you are shocked, you are slumped, you are dead weight, you are dead-lifted, you are out on the gray, you have been replaced by something sensational. Here, we do not talk. Here, we pull. Here, we kick with theatrics as if we are creating a song other than the sound of self on other—this is supposed to be sexy, this is supposed to be violent, there are supposed to be fireworks cascading: left to right, right to left, like the most beautiful fountain you've ever seen, fountains with theatrics, fire with dazzle.

Here, we must suspend belief: we must believe that these are not friends we hold dear, these are not lovers of crosses, there are no apologies for stiff slaps, and hatred spills into hatchbacks and airplanes; that we want families to fall off bridges and we have no concern; that when people leave they will not be missed, they have left at our hand, we are made of iron, and we dance on the air. That we are here to break hearts, to injure with teardrops, to create music with bruises. I never wanted any of this—I never wanted to be you: slick, small. My legs cannot kick high enough, I have broken no hearts, I cannot descend from the ceiling with a quickness to arrive at your door. My legs are not stretched. My back is strong. I cannot imagine the crush. I cannot imagine marrying a whisper. To pray as pyrotechnics surround my mouth.

I know that this loss would be beautiful. I know that I could live a life as fluid as snakes, that the vertebrae will slither and pop, that all of this deserves to be revisited someday, that there is earnestness and there are no tricks; that loss is loss; that if we could pull someone else in front of the mirror before it breaks, we would, in a heartbeat.

LET ME TELL YOU SOMETHING

Before every match, the ring announcer explains
the parameters. The default is always that the match
is scheduled for one fall—though there are five
routes to a fall. You could get pinned to the floor.
You could be in so much pain that you give up. You
could be knocked out. You could not make it into
the ring on time. You could let your emotions get
the best of you and do something illegal and get
caught. The last one happens most often—matches
get thrown out because no match exists in a bubble;
there are grudges held over from previous matches,
there is always someone watching. There is always
something to be ruined.

A Giant Is Always Interrupting

Jorge the Giant

Because when someone is the tallest person you've ever seen, you wish them taller. There is no reason to be exact in a world where we believe that a man has come back from the dead, that there are brothers born in fire, that you can put to sleep someone who has seen the other side of living. I have done this to the point where I do not know what my actual height is anymore, the same way that we are quick to answer when someone asks us our name, what city we sleep in. There is a belief that the human brain can convince itself of a lie so thoroughly that it believes it is telling the truth. I cannot remember where I heard this, so this may not be true. I do not know the term for telling the world that you are one thing when you are the other. If I am telling you a lie I believe to be true, you cannot call me a liar. Check the indentations in the mattress. Measure from the crown of the head to the floor. Let us imagine a city where the hair on your chest is real, where the top of your skull is that many inches closer to God.

Tiger Feint Kick

The secret is it's very easy to know what is going to happen.

And that is why we watch: it is easy to predict—we know the moves that are going to happen before they happen. We expect false falls, the escape from being finished. Rey Mysterio, a *lucha libre* wrestler has a move called the 619—an overly complex ritual that requires Mysterio's opponent to be draped over the second rope, facing outward, before Mysterio jumps through the second and top ropes while holding on to them and uses the momentum to swing back around into the ring, kicking his opponent in the face. The situation never arises in any other match—the helplessness of a muscle-bound superstar falling halfway out of the ring and getting caught on the ropes is rare and frankly unbelievable—so there is inevitably an absurd sequence that allows Mysterio's opponent to find himself in this predicament. The audience notices it immediately: this matter of circumstance on which, surely, Mysterio will capitalize. We are promised something is coming.

As a child, wrestling shocked me: each twist was an actual twist that I never saw coming. The superkick, the clothesline after the arm raise, the leg drop on the wrong guy. Now, the outcomes are predictable: this guy needs to win the title because the Monday night show can't have two champions, or this match is just a set up for a later match, the real one. If we are wrong in our predictions, we are pleased.

On the days after a tornado ripped through half of my town, on the days when the lights came back, and the cable came back, and the normalcy of not waking up every morning to the smell of chainsaw came back, I found myself embracing the predictable. I stopped watching basketball, as I had too much anxiety about the outcome—whether my team was going to secure the winning rebound, or not, whether they could hold home court, whether they could somehow survive and advance. Instead, I watched wrestling, the builds as apparent as the line of wreckage, the story lines laid out in front of me like the found belongings of a roofless house.

We knew the tornado was coming—there were warnings for days that the outbreak could be bad, the merging of cold and warm air hitting at the right spot to form twisters at the Mississippi border, any one of which could take a tree, a garage, a body.

But there was still hope that the line would deviate—that somehow the wind would dissipate on the air like a wisp of smoke. The real con is that they know we know. They know that we get excited when we see a villain draped over the ropes, as Mysterio bounces from one side of the ring to the other. They know that we anticipate a shin crashing, the opponent grabbing at his face as he falls backward. They know that we know what's next: Mysterio climbing to the top rope to finish him off. They know, so sometimes the villains know too: they linger a little bit too long between the ropes before ducking out of the way of the spinning kick; they put their arms up in time to catch Mysterio midspin, hoisting him up on their shoulders before driving him into the mat.

I am asked if the tornado is a monster—if it knew what it

was doing when it sucked up the water in the lake, scattered the mailboxes fifty miles away. I always say no; it simply does what we expect an act of nature to do. Who are we to judge the weather? And who are we to try to predict what is coming?

Hulk Hogan Comes to Tuscaloosa

(after J. McCall)

And it's really him; at least that's what the children say, that the sky turned red and yellow before it grew black, white thunderbolts across the sky like an interruption, a whistle on the wind that doesn't know any better. The kids would say this, of course, despite being told to stay away from windows—it is hard to make out primary colors with a mattress over your head in the center of a dark hallway. It's hard to blame them for these things: the safest place in a tornado is not outside of the ring but in the heart of your house. The recitation of passages from younger days and hypothetical disasters that you would never need: bombs can be stopped by the hard lacquer of school desks, a funnel will only lap at my shirt if I lie facedown in a divot, alligators are confused by the zigzagging of slow, scared feet.

He came to town and ran wild: a chainsaw in every hand, broken glass in every big boot. I can still tell you where everything once was, in a time when everything was laid out in front of us like it was supposed to be there. Nothing new ever comes through this town—the trains whistle before smashing into turnstiles, the bounce-back stagger of a few too many beers at a place we know without saying its name.

I am lucky in that I learn tricks quickly. The human body does not work that way—there is no way to ignore whatever pain has been inflicted upon it; a leg trapped in a steel chair can bear the weight of two men, a cutting crash can be brushed aside with the shaking of fists and the clenching of a jaw. The trick here is that my house is old: Carpeting you could lose a string of pearls in, a stove that rattles when the coils glow red. The shower head spits water against windows: whatever light is left in the sky glows through. Whatever you have heard about bathtubs and tornadoes is conditional when you are reminded that wind can peel shingles off a rooftop like cotton can be split in half by the fistful. Here, underneath, is me, not you: I do not shimmer, my skin is not the color of the sun, I do not have anything to be envious of except a soft heart and an iron will to make it out alive if the situation called for it—no one kicks out from this, there is no chance of me going over the storm, my body on the swirling wind until it is choked out into nothing; perhaps if I spin fast enough, arms out, I could dissipate all of this into stillness, that where I stand is where I stand and we will all be safe: we will continue having birthdays as they were meant to be, blankets laid out on the dying grass of April as we celebrate, leaving nothing but bottle caps and bones. That one year later, you couldn't find me on a red stool where I always sat, waiting until the clock struck something familiar—that there was nothing for us to do to celebrate except something that resembled tradition, a song on the speakers rooted in nonsense.

Instead, I remain still. Body curled up, anticipating a blow that I know I cannot get up from: I cannot be kicked in the face if I just stay down—the script cannot run its course, there is nothing to do but drag me into the spiral.

Before the surreal led to something more, you could never find me in a bathtub, my shoulders squeaking up against the sides like nothing special. There is no room for sex here, there is no room for Tinseltown and twinkle toes, no Hollywood, just the sound of something atomic. Before rehearsing roles, let me tell you a story about this room: A girl playing a bit part ripped the curtain from its rings. It crashed into the water like the pillars of something much more majestic than what will happen and has happened here: a small town turned nuclear, a map revealing a dark diagonal scar down through parts of the city we never went to. The rage here was wasted on something so unimportant; the true tragedy would be in a city that she shouted the name of every time this town felt too real.

When the hulking swirl came through, it did not deviate: later, people ask me if a monster came that day, and I am uncertain. The monsters of the city where I was born come in different forms: a mouth that spits green mist, a man waving the flag of a place I fear. I would like to tell you that I have stopped believing in monsters the same way that I have stopped believing in heroes, that every soft-closed fist hits a forehead and opens up like a magnolia. Yet they are there with every thought of something sour, how when I try to tell you the best I ever felt was after bodies were found faceup in lawns they had never been in, how plate-glass windows shattered to pebbles, how all I wanted was for someone to lick the gasoline from my fingers. How we have been broken and you treated it like an honor: to have almost been killed by the greatest trick ever pulled and to live to remember it.

This is all to say that I have been saying my prayers; that instead of counting all of the dangers that we could miss, I am living to remember; that I am cursed on nights when the wind picks up and the sky turns yellow; that I refuse to be taught what it means to be wild. There is nothing left to be said of bathtubs, of mattresses. This reckoning will never be called "brother."

LET ME TELL YOU SOMETHING

There are other stipulations. Last Man Standing.
Falls Count Anywhere. Two out of Three Falls.
Tornado Tag. Steel Cage. Battle Royal. Ladder Match.
Tables Match. No Holds Barred is the same as No
Disqualification. Loser Leaves Town. All of these
matches are meant to raise the stakes—a regular
rivalry just isn't enough, so there needs to be some
sense of finality. Wrestling, though, never stops.
There is no off-season—it expects its audience to
forget about alignments, to age out entirely. In a
world of hyperbole, there is never such a thing as
never again.

Splash

The secret is in the anticipation.

There are days my body surprises me in ways that I welcome—like when my muscles seize up and I am convinced that I will never be able to walk straight again, that each step will slap at the pavement, that the muscle sheaths won't dare glide like they once did. What I once described as a halo, I recognize as tightness—I can anticipate my body beginning to grow smaller within itself; I feel a flare-up is inevitable. I know that when I go to bed that evening, I will wake up with my ankles stiff as chain link, that I am justified in my dread, that we can feel it coming.

Those mornings when I awake in pain there is vindication—though my body seems to be unpredictable, I have found a pattern in the pain; I can feel it coming. If one is in agony, one might as well be correct in it.

To ascend to the top rope is to let the universe know that something is to be expected. The word is always "high-risk maneuver," as if to insinuate that there is a danger here that has the promise of paying out—that the wrestler is going to do something that is going to end either in victory or in failure. The truth is that the odds are always that it is going to end poorly—a splash with no water in the pool, an elbow with nobody home. A highflyer caught on the top rope before being suplexed into the middle of the ring, with both athletes lying flat on their backs after the impact. There is something beautiful about the idea of all or nothing: that either I am capable of running five-mile laps around my town or I am subjected to staying home with my foot elevated, unable to even make it to the kitchen to fix a glass of water in hopes that it will somehow wash away whatever pain I am in.

The key is that there is always something that happens—a failure of this magnitude is at least glorious in its attempt. Wrestlers either hit the move or have nothing left. A missed aerial move leaves them open for a ground-based attack; a flop that hits nothing but air and canvas can be quickly pounced upon; a bicep wrapped around a chin can knock whatever wind remained after the crash landing, as if it was foolish to ever think that one could fly this high. The risk, then, is never in the move itself but in what happens afterward: a writhing on the mat in pain, a shock of being so high before hitting the lowest of lows. Four weeks ago, I ran a marathon. I had enough in my legs to keep me upright for over twenty-six miles. I had flexion in my feet. Today, I can barely make it three miles without needing to stop, my calf muscles conspiring against the rest of my legs, my hips devoid of motion.

In wrestling, a life of excess is hated until it is rewarded; we hated Ric Flair but quote him endlessly. I tell myself it is in my best interest to be in this much pain, that it is something that I have somehow earned—that this is what I've deserved since the beginning. That if I ever find myself somewhere in the middle, I have already lost.

Ric Flair Has More Cars
Than You Have Friends

It was a champagne mess of a thing, less sheen than what would be expected from such decadence but capable of still shining bright after a soft rain and a hard scrub, time trading everything up to a newer model, the engine block knocked back a few inches after a hard left-hand turn on a changing yellow, as a man I never saw again sped through the intersection to beat the light. A hole in the grill refashioned to separate me from the other kids on my block with their tied-down hoods and their rattling mufflers, although you understand this better than most: a straight line of false whites that can cut through the flabs of fat above an eye while the rest of the world has its back turned.

It brought me here: a place where I've met too many names that I can't recall, the same way that you used to list cities where you knew women were waiting up for you; you'd repeat the names of towns but never the names of people—I always assumed that you were from one state when in actuality you were from a place where it snows in September. Deliver me here, friend, away from where headaches and blurred vision are beyond destinations, where the jewels on your back glimmer in their weight draped over your outstretched arms. You own more ways to get from city to city than I have couches to sleep on if the night goes to hell and the wind kicks up too high, money spent on spilled liquor that has evaporated like white smoke from a too-hot chassis. Yet you are never the one behind the wheel, preferring to sit in the back, glancing at your watch but not to look at the time, as the diamonds on the second hand weigh down the gears—the hours stutter in place.

This is what dreams are made of, I know, and this is every man's nightmare: to lose control of the edges, to have blood blur the line between eyebrow and cheekbone, to have our bodies keep us safe because we know how bodies work: I know that if I slap my chest it will leave a mark, that my feet will not go against my will, that they will stay cemented to the floor. A kiss that is stolen is not a kiss in the same way that none of these children are the world's: custom-made brothers and sisters, all things tailored to suit, to not be but to have been, a name that isn't ours. We all dream that we are falling: the bottom dropping out, our legs stable until they are not, flopping face first onto the floor while the crowd cheers.

In my dreams, the car does not listen, the shifting of gears marred by feet tangled in top sheets, the sensation that the open road is an iced-over lake. The car drives itself and there is no way out of the backseat. It is snowing, when the clouds say it should be impossible. The door is locked from the inside and no one is driving the car. The car rolls past the house I grew up in—all cream and blue with hedges lining the walkway, a house too small for you to even consider a home; you'd never believe me if I told you I used to sleep on a mattress in a hallway, if I told you how the crawl space made my skin itch. I saw a snake there once, though you preferred alligator. I saw a rat there once, but you would use this against me. The car door will not open, and my parents are out on

33

the front porch, waving. I pass them sixteen times and the door will not open—at least in the steel cage you can see the lock, can see how the chain is wrapped around the chain link.

I did not learn to drive until I was much older. The first day I took to the highways of my youth, past the dealerships and churches, the circles where I bore right at each and every fork, the right tire blew out, a soft jerk of the steering wheel before I could power it back away from the median. Years later, I press my face to the wind so that I can stay awake after hours of wanting to get back to my own bed—blankness finds its way through any windows if you keep them open enough, something that you have figured out after too many last matches to the point where the world apologizes before popping you good underneath your chin. You, limousine riding, jet flying, do not understand what it is to fall asleep behind your own wheel. Yet you and I know what it is like to be lost in the lights, to be shaken by brightness, to touch the center of our forehead and feel blood, to be wooed by the death of our own devices. To be who we are, we must beat someone we are not. We must let the world know that we can shake off any images of drowning, of falling backward into the silence of snow. I am awake and I have one car and three dead friends. The car has a broken windshield, a crack that started with a spit-up dead bolt on a road that shares your name. I have friends who have died in cars. I have friends who don't remember my name. I have a lot of things—some sparkle like broken glass, and others are as dull as a scraped-up hubcap. A night side table. A mouth full of ice. A dawn thus spoken.

LET ME TELL YOU SOMETHING

Boxers wear robes to the ring to keep them warm
before a jab to the right cheek will. Wrestlers
do the same, but it is more about the pomp and
circumstance—Gorgeous George taunting the fans
or Rick Rude inviting a woman to help him take
off his clothes, revealing his impossible physique
before a match. There are fewer robes these days;
instead, wrestlers wear T-shirts with their names
and catchphrases on them in an attempt to sell them
to the fans at home. The more that superstars sell
merchandise, the more likely they are to receive
airtime. Wrestlers have hawked armbands, action
figures, cereal, pillows, championship belts, video
games, *luchador* masks, ice cream bars. The selling
begins well before the bell rings.

Body Slam

The secret is the ring absorbs most of the fall.

The wrestling ring itself is constructed of wood planks and foam padding, the wood bowing with every slam, the padding and canvas softening the blow on the skin, protecting a stray splinter from getting wedged in a forearm. It has more bounce than a boxing ring, though not as much as it may seem—many wrestlers when adjusting to the WWE find themselves taken aback by the hardness of the ring, by how it doesn't give back as much as the makeshift stages of their coming-ups.

Wrestlers, though, look for ways to make everything harder: the outside of the ring, near the apron, is notorious for being the hardest part of the ring, and heels always look for kill shots. In no-holds-barred matches, wrestlers rip away the canvas and foam—they drive their opponents onto entrance ramps, into guardrails.

Another way I fell in love with wrestling is by pretending to be a wrestler myself—by practicing long speeches in front of my mirror or having *l'espirit de l'escalier* moments in my head after being humiliated, coming up with the perfect comeback long after the moment has passed me by. I would take pillows and piledrive them into my parents' mattress when they were not at home—those brief moments after school before my mother returned from her shift at the library, when I was always finding a shortcut from the complex's tennis court, over and through a drainage basement, before walking up the flight upstairs to the corner apartment we were renting and letting myself in.

I knew nothing of pretending to take punishment because what I received in school was too real: grabs at my nipples through my tight-fitting polo shirt, kicks at the back of my knee sending me sprawling forward. Instead, I would drop elbow after elbow onto something that could never fight back—a stuffed animal, a pillow in the shape of "Macho Man" Randy Savage, a pillow in the shape of a pillow. I would drive my body over and over into the mattress, feeling the springs bounce and uncoil with every drop. Every synthetic-cotton-fiber spine compressed. Every polyurethane-foam shoulder separated.

As I grew older, my parents would complain about the bed sagging a bit more than it used to, as my body grew larger and larger as it grew more and more unchecked, as the springs began to lose their shape, sticking up in parts, undoubtedly jabbing my tired parents while they slept. I, of course, thought nothing of these things as I dove over and over in sit-out powerbombs, vertical suplexes, or simple splashes, driving all of my weight downward over and over as I pictured the aggressors of the day.

This is what it means to dampen—after every slam, each spring would oscillate, trying to return to its original form, though overshooting, before resting approximately where it started. There have been measures of system decay, of how springs become less springy—they deaden after too much pressure, too many times expecting to bounce back.

I think often of how much I can absorb before I lose all elasticity—how each time my foot strikes the pavement, my calf muscle tightens, or how, back in those days in my parents' bedroom, I leapt in the air and crashed down without any thought of how things echo. The pain of the day transferred to a coil and then back, never noticing how the shape of a spring is constantly, always, spiraling downward.

Tune In to The Miz's New
Reality Show, Immediately
Following *Monday Night Raw*

Mostly because things started getting a little too real—we remember the casting call where we learn that he has a deep need to be loved, for the fights both real and simulated, for the not knowing how to talk to anyone who doesn't call your home home, for the wanting to talk with strangers on the rooftop.

To be aware of falsehood is to know what truth is, unless it all displays itself as artifice: a wooden bird standing atop a tree house, a bright light meant to wash out the imperfections on my forehead. I know of wood—of how we eliminate as much of it as possible to create something worthwhile, of how it burns when guided; birch bark ignites faster than paper some days, even though they both come from the same source, although the unprocessed bark has a harder time flying away with a strong wind off a cold lake.

What happens when we ask someone whose life has been to perform to stop pretending—do we get to see something hidden? We know some of the tricks of the eye, how there are thin pieces of plywood under the mat to break falls, but there are also razor blades tucked between fingers to more easily open up an eyebrow. I am an actor playing a fighter playing an actor playing a father—someone who has seen everything this world has to offer and deciding to take it apart; as if you can separate a life from the lights that illuminate how strong we are.

And perhaps this is why no one ever leaves this business—we parade old legends out on stage, their skin separating from the woody plant that they have become, too slick, still, to burn, too young to completely dry out. When you ask about someone from your youth, you can simply state that they are still at it, somewhere, away from where there are hard cameras and long wires—they are in dimly lit gymnasiums, centers where there are group exercise classes and middle school proms; replace the dance floor with a ring. We have the right cables for the microphone so you can hear the bold proclamations of the day—who will be king, who will leave here bloodied, who will leave here out on their feet.

Will you be following me after whatever it is I am known for? I will wake up late—I will never rise with the sun. I will walk to the kitchen—I will drink water from a glass that is cracked on the bottom. There will be days when I will leave the house; perhaps I will get a coffee, perhaps I will meet someone that I have not met yet for lunch—something much different than what I eat now, more greens, perhaps, more spinach. This is real, I will tell you, over and over again. This is how I live now. There is a birthday coming up, and someone has forgotten the cake. There is a house in disrepair. There is a child coming. It will have my eyes. I will not know what to do—I will forget the child in its crib, I will forget the child's shoes, I will forget, and I will forget, and I will forget. I will stop being polite in my absent-mindedness. I will misremember my manners. Please make sure that you are here for all of this, so you can show the world who I was, once. How well I dressed—how I coordinated my tie with my pocket square. How well I moved—how my hair looked. Of course, none of this will be real either—instead, I'll take the fall to make someone younger look better. I'll get knocked cold to make the crowd hate you in ways they never thought possible. I'm too old for this, they'll say, and they're right. There are decks that need washing. There are children to look after. There are some things that just shouldn't be seen.

LET ME TELL YOU SOMETHING

Challengers are introduced first, champions last.
Some days there are sobriquets: the Phenomenal,
the Planet's Champion, the People's Champion,
Le Champion, the All-Mighty. There are weights,
occasionally; bad guys from distant lands are
measured in kilos. There are places: Residing
in Hollywood, California. From West Newbury,
Massachusetts. From Calgary, Alberta, Canada.
From Death Valley. From Kyoto, Japan. From Truth
or Consequences, New Mexico. In the early days,
wrestlers were billed from Parts Unknown as a way
to add mystique to their characters: How can anyone
prepare for a fight when no one knows where they
are coming from?

A Giant Is Always Interrupting

*Giant Bernard's Name Has Changed
to Protect His Past*

You came back to us changed, as many do when they disappear into the oceans—even though you are on the other side of the world, the world does not stop without you; you, you are of this world whether you wish to be or not. They never mentioned your name until it was too late—a white man with kanji written down the side of your face, meticulously painted on before every street fight or shouting match where you pretend to have lost the language of your birth, how to say "champion," how to say "mine." When we are tired, we drop the act—like any good giant, you end up dancing; how funny it is to see a body like that move, your thick Atlantic accent reappearing as you forget what was once forgotten. Giants have no choice but to be made up of a sum of their parts, so I believe that you were in there all along, friend. When you are larger than the mountain that bears your name, it is foolish to think you can be everything you wish to be at once.

Omoplata

The secret is if a match is memorable, it is a victory.

A comeuppance of over ten years. He swung first, calling me a fat chicken before hitting me over the head with two textbooks, wrapped in brown shopping bags and taped to the front covers. My instincts took over: I emulated everything I saw my heroes do. I kicked him in the stomach until he doubled over. I raised my knee to his face.

I knew wrestling was fake—that if anyone caught a thigh to the face flush, they would drop like a sack of flour. I don't remember much after the blood and the girls laughing. I am still waiting for the repercussions: that swift justice will be served; that, despite all of the ducking and torment, I still haven't earned my shot; that we would drop this story line and write me off completely. In the early '90s, Jake "The Snake" Roberts tormented the Ultimate Warrior through a series of vignettes meant to toughen up the Ultimate Warrior and have him engage his "dark side" so he could take on The Undertaker. Warrior was put through hell: buried alive, surrounded by snakes, locked in a casket. It was finally revealed that Roberts never intended to toughen Warrior up—instead, he had been working with The Undertaker all along, revealing his true colors when he had one of his pythons poison Warrior and delivered him to The Undertaker to pick the bones.

Two months later, I left that school. I let a few people know that I would be leaving, but for the most part, I disappeared. I can't help but wonder if anyone ever thinks of me—and if, even though that smear of blood on my jeans was one of the most memorable moments of my life, it meant nothing in the grand scheme of things.

I've realized that I remembered the Warrior-Roberts feud incorrectly—I thought there was a definitive end when there wasn't one. I swore that Warrior took out The Undertaker, clearing the path for a showdown with Roberts. That Roberts stayed one step ahead of him, landing cheap shot after cheap shot until Warrior gorilla press slammed him until he liquefied to venom. It gives me pause that my moment of glory did not happen the way that I remember it either—I remember getting hit. I remember connecting twice, but Lord knows where, or what damage was done. Was there blood? Was I in a cafeteria or a library? You were wearing a brown T-shirt, but perhaps you weren't.

Warrior returned eventually. I did too, but to a different landscape—a pale version of what we left behind. A Saturday morning, my mother dropped me off at the same cafeteria to take the SAT. The walls were different—a new mural adorned the cinder blocks. There were new chairs too. But the smell was still there: of bleach and grease. There, too, was the same vending machine, tucked in the corner—candy bars and sticks of gum all wrapped up in the spiraling metal.

The Ultimate Warrior Believes
in Nothing but Forever

A question to answer your question: When the plane goes down or the heart goes out, do you kick the doors down or do you let everything occur as it should? A smile on the face before it twists into a chipped-tooth mess, a resignation that what is happening is happening without you: hearts work independently of bodies, hearts blink first, hearts jump off the train tracks early without seeing headlights coming the opposite way. We build only to tear things down, construct fortresses of pillows and couch cushions, our stuffed animals safe in their beds as we are—tucked in under pillowcases, their soft heads peeking out from under fabric. We crash into these structures like we are giants, like we are larger than any building that has ever been constructed: we are the unexpected reckoning, we have no time for anything delicate. And then, it is over: our lungs too tired to build again, our work in a heap on the floor. There is no time for any of this, though we believe it to be endless: our hearts in the right place for once—chest-centered and majestic, a spilling out of leaves from under the soup tureen, all things set out for us like a dinner we will never attend. Here, we live in a space between heartbeats, in a world where we try to determine what is rightfully right and wrongfully wrong with no luck: no four-leaf clover, no fingers crossed behind our backs. When we see you, you spin away from us, your back to the camera as you talk to nothing, colorful walls that you cannot see—eyes focused on the blankness of being.

You promise us that you live this: that every footstep you take, every trip to the grocery store to buy bananas for your family, every moment that you turn on a car engine, you are him, ready to destroy everything in your path, ready for warfare, your code existing on a plane that we cannot possibly comprehend, we soft of skin, we who choose to spend our days in bed counting the spirals on the ceiling. We, destroyers of buildings. We who do not sing loud enough to give you the power to shake ropes, to press men larger than we can imagine above our heads, to paint our faces the color of something not found in nature—to become larger than life, to become larger than our mothers, our fathers.

These arms are tired. These arms are pressed for time. Dispose of them. Assume the controls of a body that does not have the need for carrying. I will forget all wounds until it is time to drag you home by your teeth. A question to answer your question: To die like you did, not behind the wheel of a car, but in a house that was built by someone who could still lift Sheetrock above their heads like I did as a child— before sycamores and straight spines—to die after ceremonies, to die after you were pronounced dead—gone with no semblance of spark, no glorious send-off, but a chance to do it over—to be alive when the world is shocked you are still breathing is no easy task, and so when the plane goes down and the doors are kicked out, do you believe that you are the one chosen, plucked from on high, the neon paint a sharp contrast to the grays of cockpits?

My blood is not yours: it does not run thick, it runs silently while I sleep. I do not act on instinct. I do not throw myself face first into the void, I do not ask for forgiveness before I ask for permission. I am quiet, yet my body is failing. I cannot obliterate because I cannot love: I was never taught these things—you never spoke of love, of wishing to die for a cause until it was too late. Some nights, I drink too much. Some nights, the sky is clearer than coffee; some nights, I do not miss any of this. I show up of my own accord: the truth is inexhaustible. Don't worry about any of these things: they are minute in their crafting, they will be wiped away with the simplicity of a headfirst charge from parts unknown into the only thing I know—to be strong enough to leave everything behind except everything I stood for, to keep my name in my heart and on my sleeve like shreds of fabric. This blood does not bleed deep: no one will think I am alive when I am not. I will tell my stories. I will sing them at any cost. I will keep the spirit close. None of this will become legend.

LET ME TELL YOU SOMETHING

Some wrestlers don't wait for the bell in order to get
a jump on their opponent. In a blood feud, as soon
as the bell rings, the action is hot from the start.
Most matches, though, start with a traditional collar-
and-elbow tie-up and a series of reversals. A test of
strength. At some point, a strike is thrown: a kick to
the midsection with a stomp, a slap across the chest.
Nothing actually starts until we can hear it.

Open-Hand Strike

The secret is the true art is in taking punishment, rather than giving it.

I am inherently disinterested in violence that I know to be real. I grew up watching boxing matches with my grandfather and great-grandfather: Tuesday night fights and big bouts on pay-per-view, my grandmother calling the cable company early in the afternoon to make sure that the screen shaped up in time for the opening bell. But even then, I was more interested in the pageantry: The silk robes and walk-out music. The touching of gloves. A lunch-room fight spills out into the snow as the assistant football coaches rush to break it up before someone loses an eye.

I am not competitive by nature. I am comfortable letting others win if it means avoiding conflict. I tell myself that there is no such thing as a zero-sum game, that somehow, some way, we all can be victorious, have our hands raised at the end of something grueling.

It is harder to get yourself in position to be held than it is to hold. Something to know about me is that I never stayed down for long—I would be swarmed by smaller children with sharp elbows, and they would take turns trying to knock me over, their laughs echoing off my body at a task that they viewed to be impossible, my weight steadfast in its immovability. I learned, over and over, how to take it—that there was something rewarding in being patient rather than just a chest bruise and skin torn where a fingernail got caught.

The oft-quoted Mike Tyson has a quote that has been interpolated into every possible iteration. When preparing for a fight against Evander Holyfield, he grew tired of interviewers telling him how Holyfield was going to dance around him and try to tire him out with constant movement. Tyson replied, "Everyone has a plan until they get hit. Then, like a rat, they stop in fear and freeze."

But my plan was to get hit. Was to have every sugared-up middle schooler give me whatever rage they had. To have their knuckles hurt from too many punches to my upper arm. To demonstrate my persistence. To emerge from sleepover basements bruised but unbowed. Instead, I was the one who was frozen—to fight back would be unfair. To swing, even as a reaction, would break every single rule. The audacity of fighting back.

In professional wrestling, a closed fist is illegal. Instead, everything is open-handed. Karate chops. Palm strikes. When wrestling, we do not adhere to these rules: we know that the strikes are fake, but the momentum behind the swing is real. In a world where sending your opponent into a guardrail is legal, an open palm is an unwritten rule.

Those who lose well make an art form out of it. There's a term for this: enhancement talent. You are here to make the monster look stronger, the tactician look even more impressive. Losing well is a gift.

A Giant Is Always Interrupting

Kamala Was Born in Senatobia, Mississippi

But give a Black man a spear and he could be from anywhere: Sudan, Uganda, hell, you could put a few vowels together and make up a land the world forgot—the deepest and darkest, the parts unknown. Of course, he'd have to be brought here by someone—discovered by a man in khakis and a pith helmet, standing over his tribesman in brutal victory; you know the games they play are much more violent than the ones we play in our civilized countries, yes? We feed him scared white boys in ill-fitting trunks who could be from just down the road; they might give him a microphone for him to stammer out some small neighborhood the next town over to let us know that it could be any of us—this man, this monster, this savage has come into our town and looked at one of us one-eyed.

So when they asked a southern son to slap some white paint on his bald head and claim some unknown trampled thatch in an overgrown forest, it was a stretch, certainly, but in real towns with real boys in them, he needed not go shirtless: he could wear a polo with his college's mascot above the left breast, a T-shirt with a comic book superhero, he could wear his hood up or down, and it'd have the same effect. Fear is fear in any patch of land, and if you're scared, shout it to the moon.

Bret Hart and the Finished
Dungeons of Our Youth

Legends are born here: of sweat-soaked vinyl and broken bones, of holes in the Sheetrock, of elbows fitting into eye sockets. I am having difficulty telling you these things because of what happens to fat boys with kind hearts in basements; you could kill all of them if your heart was blacker—you could twist an arm until it popped. You could ruin all of the fun. It is a secret down here, our bellies full of corn syrup, of taunts, of how you took the biggest slice. It was your mistake to wear these clothes. You should've known that something like this could happen—fabric tearing around the neck, a scratch on the shoulder. You know this is fake, right? You know the fix is in, yes? And it is; this is not your house—your pictures are not the ones on the wall. You are underneath somewhere you've never been and this is what is expected of you—there is no room for a television in your basement, among the paint cans and saw blades. There is no room for any of this there: someone could get hurt—no carpet over concrete, just a slight sparkle among the gray.

In other dungeons, we roller-skated: we minded the load-bearing poles, we whipped around in circles when it was hot outside, when the sun was too much for us to hold. In other dungeons, we watched your excellence—your glasses were always rose colored to hide your nervousness; we learned to fear the color pink. You, off the second rope instead of the third. You with the axe handle. I, too, cannot look anyone in the eye. I, too, am afraid of heights. I, too, wish to build something stronger than who I am, instead of being ripe for the pummeling: skinny elbows striking my shoulder, and I, a dumb, soft ox not knowing how to stay down.

....

Here, underneath, there are no windows and you cannot save me: you cannot execute, you cannot aim, you cannot lock on. In a world of hulks and giants and the undead, you were the least believable—a man from a place with three names, a man in leather, a man whose claim was timeless. You, the humble hero. You, refusing to be a cowboy because you knew no stampede. You, king of the oubliette, graduate of the dungeon.

Here is a promise that I can keep: I will return to the basements of my youth. I will reclaim the walls. I will pretend to understand what this all means: That to be under something is more than to be something, that here I can be a king, that here I can be a monster with wings and skull teeth. I can be timeless. That when the children jump from staircases onto my back I can shrug them off, grab the back of my back and stumble into a corner to buy myself some time before coming back with a quickness. That I can tell a story with these aches, that I am pretending I am hurt when I am not. These children, they watched you too: I have seen how they shield their eyes; I have seen how they turn good men bad. Nobody in the building cares, yet everyone knows that I cannot be heartless; that I cannot break your back like a pendulum. I cannot tell you that your brother will be dead in ten months.

I cannot tell you that this will end suddenly. I cannot tell you that this wasn't all part of the plan.

When I come to, I am standing over you: your legs locked, your back twisted, your head being ground into the carpet. It is your birthday; there are photos to be taken, there are cupcakes to be brought into school on behalf of you making it this far. The floor is burning your cheek. You have given up and I refuse to hear the bell. Wrestling is not real. The blood vessels in your eyes have burst. If I could just get home. If I could just survive the night. If I could put them all to sleep. None of this is real. If I could just get home. You cannot pretend that you have won, that there is a bell ringing, that you are the champion of anything. None of this is real: we have no time for finishing. All of the houses have been sold—the machines disassembled, the walls patched. I now live in a place where there are no basements—what we are left with are concrete slabs, pits of red clay, single stones holding the weight of timber. There are no holes. There are no crawl spaces where secrets live.

Yokozuna and the Calling of
Names That Aren't Our Own

It was the right ocean but the wrong island—instead of rising suns, there was the son of islanders: wild-eyed and wild-isled, grunting instead of using words, every syllable guttural, every bark signifying a smash. The monster was billed from Polynesia in hopes that we would ignore geography and the limiting stretch of triangles across Oceania and concentrate on him—thick-nosed and stoic—a body so wide it looked as if it touched both guardrails as he lumbered away from something much more majestic than where he was hailed from: a certainty where there should be mystery, fistfuls of salt being mistook for granules of sugar. He eats the dough anyway, shoveling the mush into his mouth despite claims of it tasting terrible, despite having no need for any of this. He is an eater of men, swallower of everything.

The story goes that a wrestler tied a rope around his waist and dared any man to touch it. To come close enough to the man is to show some strength that cannot be found in smallness: your arms must be larger than legs; there is something there that two hands cannot be wrapped around. The story continues: he was the best—other men had tried to move his mass, to send his swollen body out of the circle, to make anything but the soles of his feet touch sand.

It is my turn to tell you a story. I never wanted to be you, but I was you: the biggest kid you've ever seen, the one whom all size was measured by. The champion of taking up space: every chair a challenge, every bottom of a desk pressed up against the tops of my thighs. I do not view chairs like you do: see how I spill out, see how I am held captive by the confines of skin.

You did me no favors. You, silent as they come: let the skinny man speak for you, let the only noise be when you run—the wheeze of a man on his back. They called for a forklift when I hit the ground, suggesting that I could not lift myself up—that I would dare try to move this mass I created. They would push me to watch me teeter like a sad oak, thinking that the momentum would send me spiraling, that if I could not control what I ate I could not control my entire body—that what rested in my stomach and on my tongue spoke for these legs, these knees.

There is a story about both of us: if you cut us open—if one of those brown-eyed boys with elbows for days could pin either of us to the ground and take the knife across our chest—we would spill out gravy, we would leak chocolate syrup, what would cascade out of our bodies and down our bellies would be anything but blood, anything that would make us seem anything like a human. They do not know how to prepare us because they do not eat anything, their mothers offering cupboards while they push noodles shaped like our tongues around their plate, each fork prong squeaking as it rubs against the porcelain, the remains on the dishware brushed off into the trash can before the dishes are loaded into the sink. They do not know to strangle us: to press their fingers into the softness of our necks, to push our chins up into our cheeks. You do this to keep our blood inside of us. You do this to crush us for once: to cut our arms from our shoulders, to spin the gold wheel, to press us like a dead duck, to have us gush marrow.

I will tell you a secret beyond the ones you know: the cane to the back, the death in the cameras. We all have our weaknesses, and here is mine: Wipe the salt from your eyes and smear it on my skin until I grow thin, tough. My cheeks will shrivel to leather—I ask that if you are going to make me into nothing, I will be a nothing you cannot chew. Do this before I pin you down with my weight, before I will be more than you can ever carry. Here, it does not matter where I am from: there is no air in your chest that will allow you to say even the name of the smallest island. Save your breath: I am trying to give you back your sweetness.

Owen Hart and the Finite Life of Ropes

This is not a part of the entertainment here tonight. This is not for you to enjoy—this is not for you to think about in terms other than the ones that I am presenting to you now; this is not a part of the entertainment here tonight. I repeat, this is not a part of the entertainment here tonight. Please be patient with us: we have just seen a man separate chest from heart—we have seen a man fall from the rafters. This is not an angle. This is about a straight drop from a height unthinkable: we will look to the ceiling and count the cross-beams—the metal catwalks, the rattle of metal. You should have never been up there. This is not about angles.

When they tell the story, they say that your head hit the turnbuckle where the ropes meet the post—that your head flew clean off, that there were people with your blood on their faces. That you staggered like a dying bird, that we were all horrified. That there was glamor here: that there is beauty in a man falling in a blaze of blue before his jaw and his neck separate, that you were killed as loudly as you spoke, that there was something poetic here—I remind you that this is not a part of the entertainment here tonight—that your neck cracked the same way you cracked another man's, spine jammed up until it topples. I have the unfortunate respon-sibility to let everyone know that this is not how a man dies, this is not how the towel is thrown in, this is not part of the entertainment here tonight, this is not a part of the show. This is not a lot of things.

They never show the body hitting: the grip is lost on the knuckle, the cable does not hitch, and the body disappears from view like a balloon cut from a toddler's grip; it swirls on the air but rises until we mistake it for a star, until we imagine that the nylon bursts from the height. We imagine the rain falling in reverse, coming up from the ground, trickling up our calves and under our arms, drops flicking themselves off the tips of our follicles. If I believe in gravity, I believe that we can fall forever, that there is no such thing as a force that can break bodies. I have the unfortunate responsibility to remind you that you did not die like he did, neck broken, quietly in a hot garage, folding chair kicked out from underneath your legs. This is not an angle. This is not part of the entertainment. There is no sound for a chest snapping, a line drawn across a heart, a way to make this look more real.

When you stop breathing, all that you have been is forgotten in all that you become: a reason to hold hands, a ghost to pray for. A tribute in name only, heart king, a name meant for you but assigned to someone else—a name within my own. This is not part of the show, but it always will be: every zip line, every rappel downward from a dark place higher than our heads, every telephone cable will remind me of something more than wires twisted together to become something stronger than what they are apart.

This is not part of the entertainment, but I cannot help but entertain the idea of cables snapping when they shouldn't: yours should've held taut, your body dangling in a gentle spin. His should've snapped: it is unfair to have someone you love like a brother stop breathing while inches off the ground.

The only thing your children will know of you is films

of you pretending to be serious—pretending to be wronged by birthright, by being introduced to this world later than others. They will have this too: grown men reciting poetry about burning, wet pillows, hands around throats—forgive them, the strongest do not know how to avoid metaphors for choking—their hearts are large.

Forgive me, too.

Forgive me for trying to make this beautiful when it isn't, for trying to speak when I am not ready, for faulty attachments, for making sure the rope is snug around the neck, for swapping stories about your death instead of about the jokes we shared in basements.

Please know I keep looking for you. When I say your name I never touch my heart. I never point toward the sky.

PART TWO

LISTEN TO
THIS CROWD

Kimura Lock

The secret is a match is supposed to build on itself.

I am quick to forget that my body is connected in ways that I cannot even begin to comprehend. To have a body is to be aware of its shortcomings—how my back hurts after sitting in a hard chair, how my stomach hangs low over my waist. My wife and I talk about the miracle of medicine: how we take a painkiller by mouth, swallow it, and it somehow travels to whatever ails us. It travels up to our sore throat. It finds its way to a calf muscle that refuses to unclench.

A properly applied wristlock does not affect the wrist. Our hand is grabbed and twisted, but our wrist joint does not allow for a rotating motion. Instead, the torque is sent to the forearm, then the shoulder. It is acknowledged that attacking the wrist is only meant to transition into something more: the fingerless gloves that most MMA fighters use have a practical purpose—they stabilize the wrist to prevent destabilization.

All submissions in professional wrestling are dragged out for dramatic effect. Valiant babyface heroes will almost never tap out or surrender—if anything, they will pass out or be deemed too injured to continue, demonstrating that despite being in the clutches of the monster, they will never give up. Cowardly heels will tap almost immediately after being finally caught in the clutches of the good guys, further demonstrating that they are weak of spirit. How we tolerate pain demonstrates how good-hearted we truly are.

I believe I have a high threshold for pain, although this is something that I cannot test. I have no idea what pain is supposed to feel like—all things are entirely relative. I have a body that is constantly in discomfort, although I would hesitate to call it pain. As I relax, I find myself fidgeting constantly. I feel my muscles begin to seize up, so I take a short walk, until the pain subsides and my feet start to ache. I have days when I am in so much pain that I have difficulty walking, although, again, I do not know how this compares to anyone else's chronic physical suffering. I feel a slight scratch in the back of my throat and I am constantly swallowing, if only to test it, in hopes that it will altogether disappear.

The kimura lock is named as such because the man who used it, Masahiko Kimura, broke Hélio Gracie's arm when he refused to tap out. Some choose to call it by its original name: the double wristlock. Some call it a reverse keylock. Some call it a reverse Americana. It is rumored that the Gracie family gave the move its proper name; if we are felled by something it must have some importance, be something noble. We give names to what breaks our bones.

When I watch a legitimate fight, I am surprised at how quickly the pain washes over the fighter in peril. The surrender comes suddenly, and the hold is immediately released. While I am sure the pain is unimaginable, it is believed that to tap out is to show a sign of respect to your opponent: you are in an unwinnable situation and your foe can break every bone in your arm and separate your shoulder if they so choose. Hélio's grandsons have a saying in their gym: six days if you tap, six months if you don't.

In professional wrestling, sometimes the pain is not enough. When Brock Lesnar returned to wrestling after his stint in UFC, he brought with him the kimura lock, cinching it in on unsuspecting authority figures and lesser wrestlers that needed to be written off of TV for a while. We knew that they were too kind to ever tap out, so Lesnar would wrench the arm in a way that made it seem as if he snapped every bone: a cascade from wrist to shoulder. His opponent would be wheeled ceremoniously to the back, writhing in pain. This is what we get for holding on for so long. This is what we get for trying to work through it.

Everyone Has a "Macho Man" Randy Savage Impersonation

But the key is in the quiet moments—the low register where it seems like an urgent whisper telling you, "Get out" or "Let's get out of here" or "You won't be so lucky next time." Yet so much is made of the shouting, thick with gravel—neck strained to the point where you can see the lines bulge out, each vein a road map: highways, riverbeds, the part where the mountain rises too high to go around it.

I am good at impressions. I can capture cadences—I can match pitch for pitch, I can visualize the notes being hit and scoop my voice until I match the color, indigo blending into purple. My grandmother drops all of her *r*s. Wonder. Grandmother. Murder. My mother, a softened version of being a daughter of someone, of being removed from birthplaces and horse races, of boardwalks, of the ocean. My wife, a Minnesotan, the swallowed *l*, the long vowel, the round *o* in her accent. My town, mumbled sweetness—an accent that everyone tries and no one gets right, more Carolina than Alabama. More Virginia. More brisket than pork. Less vinegar. More salt.

My name is my name here, but I say it with a slow slide as if it is a car with no ability to brake—it syrups to a halt when I'm asked for a name for the reservation, something to call out when the table is ready. I keep the end short: -ian into -ine—brine, as if my time here has been put into a mason jar and left on a shelf, submerged in salt and sugar. As if I have been softened, infused with the humidity and whatever gets stuck to the air—smoke, the scent of rubber from the tire plant, burnt pines from a summer storm a few weeks back.

There is a rumor that the man we love to pretend to be strained his vocal chords to the point of tearing—another instance of a body never holding up as it should; that by the end he was all whisper and slur; that he would grab the microphone not to show his dominance but out of necessity— no one could hold it close enough to pick up the boasts. If you say you're the cream of the crop but no one hears you, the harvest was scythed for naught—all chaff and no wheat.

But Lord, how I loved to be you to the point where I, too, changed my name when I spoke it out loud—I have been speaking in jest. I have lost what it is to say something and mean it. I wear bright colors. I speak your words, but in my voice, to let the world know that I know who you are; that I, too, stayed up past my bedtime to see if you would do the impossible, because I did not know how these worlds worked just yet; that the cards have been set since spring; that you are past time to rise to the top. I spent my dollar on long strings of meat and tried to snap them between my teeth, even though I wanted something sweeter. I bought sunglasses to hide my eyes even though the world became a blur the second I took off my glasses, but at least I could pretend to see.

And when I picture myself leaving this earth, I imitate you, too. My heart giving out without any notice—my car slowing to a stop only miles from my home. I can never match your pitch, but I can match your cadence—of speeding up and slowing down for emphasis. All impersonations end in silence: we clear our throats, we drink a glass of water, we go back to what we say and how we say it—we talk about our day, who we saw.

There are days when there is nothing left to say—there are hours where I do not say anything at all: the sun goes down and my wife is asleep. So much of our lives are spent in silence—as a child I thought death meant remaining as still as possible for all of eternity, not saying a word. Reincarnation doesn't have to exist, but bring me back to something more than a whisper. Let me be reborn in his image: all pomp and tassel. Give me circumstance for once.

LET ME TELL YOU SOMETHING

The average age of people who watch wrestling on television is fifty-four years old. Many people regard wrestling as something for children— an activity that everyone eventually ages out of. For almost two decades, wrestling has tried to cultivate a younger fan base, relying heavily on social media and YouTube and pushing kid-friendly superstars. However, the power of nostalgia and the money that comes from it proves too strong: aging wrestlers are trotted out to remind viewers of their youth and how invincible we all once felt.

Lateral Press

The secret is most professional wrestling is a television show about professional wrestling.

I would hear stories of these men—of long, drawn-out matches, of feats of strength, of crawling to the ropes screaming in agony. It was then that I started to watch wrestling, although it seemed distant—my mother would take me to the grocery store and I would pick out a VHS tape of a pay-per-view long rendered obsolete. I would watch matches out of order—I had difficulty figuring out why best friends were now bitter enemies or why the crowd was booing my former favorite relentlessly.

As I got older, tape trading became part of the mystique of being a fan. Friends would tape matches and pay-per-views off of their televisions and bring them to school the following Monday so that everyone could catch up on everything. The beautiful thing about wrestling is that it can never truly be spoiled—most of the story lines can be ascertained through a logic of how the television show works: that nothing major is going to happen in the weeks leading up to a large event; that the weekly television shows that give away matches for free are there simply as advertisements; that shows on Monday are there to hype up the larger events on Sunday nights. Instead, wrestling is told through folktale—an explanation of the twists and turns of a match can sometimes be more entertaining than the actual feats being performed in the ring. The ideas are always solid, but the execution can be lacking. The wrestling, at times, is the least important part of the story.

Today, I find myself watching wrestling on tape delay. As a child, I would stay up late to watch *Monday Night Raw*; it was such a priority that I would forgo other responsibilities—social events, after-school programs—in order to make it back to my small television in my room, turning the red cable box to 042 in time for the main event. Now, I keep the shows on my DVR and watch them long after my wife goes to sleep—I fast-forward through the slow parts, matches that don't interest me, or matchups that I've seen a hundred times over. I flip to football games, basketball games, other things that I feel like I should be watching live; wrestling will always wait for me. I am less concerned with missing something than I once was. In middle school, missing one undercard throwaway match meant the end of the world, and now, it means nothing.

There are moments where I feel outside of my body—I catch my reflection in a mirror and I believe myself to be a separate entity. There are many times when I go through the motions of the day—I teach a class on the language of time, I walk across campus for a cup of coffee—and I am not present. I have spent too many years of my life in front of screens, to the point where I view my own life through one. I dream in third person. My memories exist somewhere between my viewpoint and that of the world's. Perhaps this is because of my self-conscious nature, how I feel as if the world is always looking at me and the space that I take up, so it is only natural for me to do the same—to be forever present in how I move but not why I move.

Wrestling, of course, exists beyond television. There are live events with no recordings except for fan-captured footage. Countless matches were recorded with a Handycam by someone in the audience and then duplicated on thick black cassette tapes and sold at the flea market across the river from my house. The WWE has become aware of this: they embrace the idea of found footage where backstage altercations are constant. The universe exists outside of what we see—we can reminisce about the lockers in our high schools, but we can choose to neglect what went on inside of them: the wobble of thin plates of steel when they are bounced off the center of a forehead when swung violently open.

When independent wrestlers make their way to one of the larger organizations, there is a learning curve—not because the wrestlers are seen as incapable but because they are not used to being filmed at all times. As a result, they don't know where all of the cameras lie—which direction to turn when hitting a move deserving of a large audience. Newer wrestlers will hit their finishing maneuver and realize that their positioning in the ring is wrong. They will awkwardly jump over the prone body in order to make sure that they are facing the hard camera, as if to signal that none of this counts unless someone can see it and that they are seeing it the way it is meant to be witnessed. In these moments, we are most aware that the whole fight is for show, that wins don't mean anything if you can't see the face of the victor.

In those moments when I find myself outside of my body, I always notice how slowly I am moving—whether that is on a long run or even in something as basic as getting out of bed after a long night's sleep. I am uncertain as to which aspect of myself is the one working at the speed it is supposed to—whether my mind is well ahead of my body or there is a delay in how my thoughts react to how I move. There is an odd comfort, though, in how I am constantly watching myself; how on a good day it can be called hyperawareness; how a part of me is constantly behind, but another part of me is always gaining ground.

The WWE Hall of Fame Does Not Exist

An Inauguration Poem

It never truly has: no brick-and-mortar building built by the hands of men that you and I might never see again, silence where there should be the scraping sounds of caulk over tile, two men carrying a pane of hand-blown glass to keep children like me from touching the feathered robes of men who carried themselves like kings. Instead, there is an unmarked building that holds everything: every broken table, every piece of barbed wire used to snag a skull, every grandiose set that has become outdated and needed to be replaced. There is nothing to be put on display—no need to highlight anything anymore, no track lighting—we give in to the hum of halogen lights, we assume that there is nothing worth keeping underneath the tarps.

There is no semblance of you there: it is simply words and things you can claim—a footnote when your name is brought up, a fact brought up with a laugh and the shake of the head. The tie you wore when you got put on your back was presumably thrown out—you have no need to wear the same thing twice and can never understand why anyone would; all things are disposable, no time to hold anything dear. When a ladder breaks, we get a new one.

We speak your name on these grounds because you let a Black man with a gold heart take the bumps for you before sliding in to get your hand raised. We speak your name on these grounds even though you did not have the patience to take the prize yourself: the clippers you used to shave your opponents' heads are on a rotating platform in the sky, while the other four hands get sliced open with the safety off.

We can laugh about this because wrestling isn't real. We knew that there was no way you were going to lose the match—there are simply things that outsiders are unwilling to do; we leave that to the professionals, the ones that can afford to let their hair grow long behind the ears just so someone else's hands can take the follicles down to the scalp. We use the term "battle" loosely now. We do not have a word for "professional" anymore. We have lost the names for a lot of things because all things should be predictable; a man simply does not allow himself to be tangled up in the ropes—a body will not allow itself to drown; when a body begins to burn with its own breath, a mouth will find a way to the surface with a new name and a word thought lost to the ages.

Years later, they blew up the limousine of the man you bested: we saw the tailored pant leg go in, the door slam shut, the car catch on fire. They filmed the scene backward: the long, live walk cutting to pretaped footage; a puddle of water in the corner appearing like magic; an error in continuity. They left the husk of the car in the parking lot for effect—someone else will get rid of it, there is always a new car. You called his daughter to see if he survived the ordeal: a man of his stature simply does not go up in flames with the world watching. You were not in on the joke—you, the leader of the carnival, you who weighted the milk bottles, you, distracted by the crack of pyrotechnics. You, forgetting the first rule—if you see something it is meant to be seen. You, forgetful.

One day they will put a name on the building where we have kept everything that is worth keeping. Someone will engrave the dates, the cities, the arenas. There will be double doors that swing open. A woman will take tickets from behind a glass window. There will be holograms, gold belts on display, chairs bent into triangles. There will be videos to help us remember—the prelude to the spear, you climbing the steps.

If I am alive, if we are alive, I will bring my children. We will walk among the exhibits; we will buy all the bloated balloons, we will share a bucket of popcorn, heavy with the weight of butter. They will point at the burnt door, the tires blown out from the heat. They will ask me if I remember that day and I will tell them it wasn't real, it never existed. They will point and tell me that it is here in front of us, blackened from the smoke. I will remember and I will remember and I will remember. A kernel will get stuck underneath my gums. We will hear a scream and the sound of glass breaking. We will shield our eyes from the shards. Everyone will cheer: we all love a broken window regardless of who goes through it. The children are scared and want to go home. We will not visit the gift shop—we will not commemorate, for we are not champions and we have lost our masks. I will tell them that I am sorry for bringing them here, that we unfold the metal legs of the table just to break the wood. I will not tell them that there are no buildings that can hold this. I will not whisper that the museum is everywhere. I will not tell them that there are always new bodies. I will tell them that we own every single thing that happened to us—that every turnbuckle pad untied is written in the stars by the ghost of the season. That everything broken is worth holding on to, to remind us that there are no such things as legends.

LET ME TELL YOU SOMETHING

The Attitude Era and the wcw Monday Night Wars
served as background for many coming-of-age
stories, including mine. Wrestling, in all of its forms
is a throwback; it reminds us of the times of carnival
sideshows and not knowing which punches are real.
It takes us back to an age of disbelief—of when we
wanted to be fooled.

A Giant Is Always Interrupting

The Statue of Giant Baba Suplexing a
Sedan Was a Temporary Installation

The myth of monument is that it is an artifact: those un-earthed marble figures and hair perfectly swirled and white have given every other tribute a good name, as if there were no such thing as an ode. To remove a statue is to claim that something never happened—as if history can be erased with a hammer that isn't metaphorical; that those with a heart for demolition all of a sudden find beauty in architecture, in art, in how we can take rock and make it smoother, bronze and make it angular, to create something to celebrate the damage dealt.

Seated Senton

The secret is you either have the look or you don't.

I learned to love wrestling when I was able to take control of everything: I could build champions out of comedic relief, I could give a beloved midcarder a championship push. But what I loved most about the game is that it was entirely customizable—I could make Mankind have a Diva's entrance. I could give everyone a feather boa, a spiked vest. But most of my time was dedicated to creating a digital version of my-self—me, if I were a wrestler, scrolling through menus and options until I became my best self, one that could pull off moonsaults and gorilla presses, that could run the ropes better than anyone has ever seen.

To rebuild yourself as an avatar requires an awareness of what your body does not have. There is nothing in the menu that reminds me of me besides the length of my hair, the color of my eyes. The body sizes are relegated to numbers: 0 for the smallest, 7 for the largest, the Yokozunas, the Rikishis, the Samoans, who bring only girth and the promise of crushing their opponents with pure heft. I am fifteen years old and a 6 on a good day. But I imagine my future self— how I picture myself in ten years—inevitably slimmer with more muscle definition. A solid 2, maybe a 3, with biceps larger than the polygons can handle—my forearms clipping through my shoulders. Wrestlers fight shirtless for a multitude of reasons—to show off their physiques, to make sure that the sweat doesn't stick to their clothing under the hot lights. In the days when this was all real, it was done to show that you had nothing to hide—that there was no body armor to absorb a blow, no knife in a waistband.

I have plenty to hide.

My digital self still wore a shirt—despite the imaginary hours I dedicated to making myself something that I am not, I would still hold on to some semblance of my past: sleeping in a T-shirt on the hottest Alabama nights, wearing my bar clothes into the pool as everyone drunkenly strips down to nothing. I would tell people I sunburned easily, which meant nothing when the sun wasn't going to rise for another three hours. Wrestlers perform in clothing to protect themselves— if they have gained weight, they switch to unitards and long pants. But when wrestlers wear their gear long enough, it becomes a part of them. John Cena wears jorts and sneakers even though fashion styles have evolved. Roman Reigns is unrecognizable without his chest plate. There are parts of the past that are meant for holding on to.

The game itself is entertaining but gets repetitive. When you've figured out the secrets—running around the ring to force a count-out, the timing of the button mash—the game becomes rote. I've spent hours imagining and less time fighting: changing my hair to green, giving myself a bicep tattoo of a snake. The self you create still needs to move. The self you create is still confined to the rules of the world.

I Am the GIF of the White Kid with My Fist in the Air When the Nation of Domination Walks Out

In the old days, every fighter with Black skin was a good guy, high-fiving every open white palm, teaching kids like me to do the dance the right way even though every step was in excess. They did this so the crowds wouldn't turn ugly, throwing beer bottles at heads, turning a slur into a deafening chant. Violence toward bodies unlike mine used to be a liability. They win the right way but never grab the brass ring. A standing ovation that eventually goes quiet.

I can afford to be the bad guy because I can take these gloves off. I can lower my fist and keep it in my pocket. A black heart. A white sheep. Enough is enough, until I've had enough. This is what my solidarity looks like—what it is until I am too tired to think about these things anymore. I can take a loss knowing I'll always get my win back, can lose clean and stay at the top of the card.

They find me in the crowd as if to say everyone is doing it, the same way that we white folk scan the room for an approving nod when we try on the culture: a reference that we want to show that we know rather than actually knowing anything. I'm telling you this because I've got a recipe you just have to try. I will watch your face as you chew, and you will be kind enough to tell me it is good, not because it is but because you know my hunger for approval is something that gets good people thrown face first into the concrete.

If there's one thing I know, it's that I am obsessed with knowing: how the villain dies before the trailers start, which faction member is going to get shot in the back first. I say I knew that was going to happen almost as often as I don't, but I don't want to act surprised. I am often surprised and not at the same time. I know that every fighter can't be angry forever. I know that it eventually leads to dancing, to trying on a preacher's voice, to being what I expect you to be. To defaulting to something familiar. All my life is familiar.

When I am told I'll never know what it is like being you, I'll try my damnedest to prove you wrong. I have read the book, see? I know what that word means. I've lived here too. We got beat up in the same school, hip-checked into the same lockers. I grew up with the same things you did. I sang along to the same songs you did, though my tongue does not move fast enough to stop myself from saying words I shouldn't. You are walking down to the ring with your fist held high and I am too. This is a shared experience, yes? I cheer so loudly for you from the crowd. Tell me you hear me.

I am ready for the hot tag. I will stand there, arms stretched out as far as they can go, although you and I know I could always stretch a little farther. I will stamp my feet as you crawl toward me, only to get pulled back into the center. I will throw my hands up, discouraged. I am incapable of being hissed out of the building by simply walking through it, because men like me don't have to change our names. Instead, let me stand in the mezzanine. The nosebleeds will work too, but make sure that you can see me. Make sure they know I'm there.

Here's what I can do: I can dance poorly and everyone will lose their minds. I can stick my arms out and bobble my head with zero rotation. I can tell you what you mean to me. I sing you. Tell me I understand. Tell me how good I am.

The next time the show comes to town, you'll see me again. I'll have moved on to new favorites. They'll look like me, or they won't. They'll have long hair, biceps almost as large as the weight I ask you to carry. Because I am me, I'll want to be them, instead of simply showing my solidarity from the rafters, fist full of popcorn while I watch you get bloodied. I'll take the loss exceptionally well. I'll have made a sign with permanent marker: the colors will smudge the outside of my hand like a bruise. My arm is growing tired. I never give the ink enough time to dry.

LET ME TELL YOU SOMETHING

There is a belief that any reaction is a "good reaction"—if a wrestler is booed for any reason, the brass considers that character effective. When a character turns heel, or goes "bad," it is always blamed on the fans—they did not appreciate the craft enough, or the wrestler spent too much time trying to please everyone rather than caring for himself. The WWE does not use the word "fans"; it uses the word "you." In wrestling, there is always someone else to blame.

There Will Be No Mention of
_____'s Name Tonight

Here is what you need to know: _____ killed his wife and
seven-year-old son in their own home. _____'s wife, Nancy,
was found in an upstairs family room with her hands and
feet bound and blood pooled underneath her skull. _____'s
son, Daniel, was found dead in his bed. Autopsy reports determined that both victims died of asphyxiation. Speculation
was that _____ killed them using his own finishing maneuver, the Crippler Crossface, a modified neck crank where
_____ would wrap his hands around his victim's face and
neck, applying pressure to the throat and shoulders. This was
not true: Nancy was strangled by a cord while _____ pressed a
knee into her back. _____ heavily sedated Daniel with Xanax.
_____ left a copy of the Bible by his body. _____ committed
suicide by creating a noose from the end of a cord on a pull-
down-cable weight machine. _____ was found hanging from
the pulley cable. The official press release read, "World Wrestling Entertainment is deeply saddened to report that today
_____ and his family were found dead in their home. There
are no further details at this time, other than the _____ family
residence is currently being investigated by local authorities.
Tonight's Raw on USA Network will serve as a tribute to

_____ and his family. WWE extends its sincerest thoughts and prayers to the _____ family's relatives and loved ones in this time of tragedy." _____'s entrance music was named "Rabid." _____ disappeared from the canon but not until it was discovered that he had committed a double murder. They should've seen the signs: _____ was the only man who would take chair shots to the back of the head. _____ is the pause when undersized wrestlers are asked to list their influences, the people they loved to watch when they were growing up, the ones they wanted to be like. _____ is a word that is not allowed to be said on air, and here are a few others: belt, strap, shot. _____'s signature maneuver was a diving headbutt. _____ was kind and kept to himself. _____ was a man who killed two people. _____ was remembered fondly. The day after _____'s death, there was a tribute show with his greatest matches: the triple threat, the wire-to-wire rumble win. Other wrestlers spoke openly about what _____ meant to them. The day after that, _____ was redacted. _____ is what we think of when we think of roid rage, of snapping. _____ is why they don't show blood anymore, why when someone is split open the hard way, the referees put latex gloves on—there's a fear that whatever made _____ kill his family could be transmitted by blood, leak through our pores, sting our eyes. _____ is why wrestling is not for children, why family members ask me when my younger cousins are going to grow out of this stage—when they are going to stop trying to make each other submit to headlocks in the basement. _____ had a strange sense of humor. _____ is why nothing looks real anymore, as if it looked real in the first place, why we reserve the chairs for gut shots and slaps on the broadsides of backs. You could've predicted this. We all could have predicted this—everything in this industry is premeditated. Fourteen hours before they found the bodies of _____ and his family, an anonymous source on Wikipedia posted that _____ missed his championship match because his wife died. The source posted it as a joke, an awful coincidence. Wrestlers fall a certain way before the Phoenix splash, the *topé con hilo*. One man must lose so another man can gain. We all get our wins back after a tough loss. Wrestling is a joke full of awful coincidences. _____ felt he wasn't safe. _____ would drive down back roads to the gym. _____ would triple-check his alarm system. Friends called _____ "Houdini" because of his tendency to disappear. Another word for the *topé con hilo* is the suicide dive. _____ had no skills outside of wrestling. _____ was going to open up a wrestling academy in Atlanta, Georgia, where he would teach students to wrestle in his image. _____ sent multiple text messages that read, "My physical address is 130 Green Meadow Lane, Fayetteville Georgia. 30215." _____ sent multiple messages that read, "The dogs are in the enclosed pool area. Garage side door is open." _____ was concerned about the dogs. Nancy was killed on Friday evening between 11 P.M. and 1 A.M. Daniel was murdered on Saturday morning. _____ killed himself on Sunday evening. _____ stayed in the house with the bodies. _____ tried to book a flight to go wrestle—to pretend to cause pain to another man while making sure that he was, in fact, not hurt. _____'s real life name is _____. In the dead of night, I stopped for gas outside of Fayetteville, Georgia. I read the signs. The sun had gone down. I thought to myself, this is where _____ killed his family. This is the exit _____ took to get to the airport to catch a flight to Houston, to headline a pay-per-view, to embark on a European tour where they would pronounce his last name correctly: they wouldn't pronounce the hard *T*; it would trail off in the air like a sunset. _____'s wife's wrestling name was Woman. On the day WWE opened up its digital archive service, I searched for _____. No results were found for that term. Please try a new search. I checked the spelling, making sure I did not flip the vowels, that everything seemed in place. They confuse the letters in my name too. You can still find _____'s matches if you know where to look: if you knew he main-evented WrestleMania XX, if you remembered he was the mystery partner during WarGames. I know where to look. WWE doesn't use the word "war" anymore. Before his matches, a disclaimer reads that "WWE characters are fictitious and do not reflect the personal lives of the actors portraying them." _____ was an actor playing the role of _____. If you search your own name, _____, no results will be found for that term. What is it to search for something and find it? This could be any woman found bludgeoned to death in her own bedroom. This could be any body found. _____ could be you. _____ could be your name—this is the beauty of never existing, of being redacted. My name is _____. _____'s real name is _____. My dogs are in the enclosed pool area. In the world that we would like to imagine, Woman and Child are still alive. They never met a man named _____. The child would be named something else: named after a father who is not _____, another man, who would not grab his bicep to see if the muscles of puberty were beginning to set in. The triple threat becomes a singles match. The story is rewritten to reflect this, yet there is no alternative story because _____ does not exist. This is the story that has always been. You and I could live in a world where wrestlers could still take chair shots to the back of the head, to the temple. We could be heroes here. We could fill up our tanks and leave. We could leave garage side doors open. The dogs are free. We cannot predict what will happen. We do not know which facts will be false and which will ring true in our ears like the high-pitched whir after a blackout. What a world this would be. What a world we could create. I search your name. It comes up blank.

LET ME TELL YOU SOMETHING

Wrestling companies rely on their fans to be in on the con but to also accept that the company knows what is best for the audience. It is like any other fan relationship: there has to be simultaneously a sense of trust in the direction of a television show or football team and a healthy amount of skepticism, where the audience feels like they know better than those in charge. Our world is filled with fan-fiction message boards and *Madden* draft simulations. Where it differs from those is that a live audience can affect a story line in real time: companies will often try to force a wrestler upon the crowd, someone they have deemed to be the chosen one, and "push" him into the main-event scene. If the company is not getting the reaction it wants, it can choose to either rewrite things on the fly or risk the entire show being hijacked.

A Giant Is Always Interrupting

Before We Saw Nia Jax's Body,
They Only Showed Her Eyes

Every giant turns into a joke at some point: Have you heard the one about how the big girl tries to find love? Or the one about how the secret admirer turns out to be your former best friend looking for blood? You and I know where this is going. You were more than the universe bargained for, and we should have been in debt to you. Instead we pretend that the way you carry yourself doesn't exist. I, too, have been a floating head, cropped so you can't see the fullness of my cheeks—something I did to myself over and over as if to say "Hide the rest of me in the margins." We can talk about the beauty in mystery, but we all know humor is in the surprise— as if to say "You've been fooled." How I wanted to crush them under the weight of all that I am, even though I didn't receive the benefit of my own affirmation. In the meantime, give me anything except the weight of a leg across a collarbone. But in the meantime, you bet your ass I'll take it. All I ask is that, at some point, you let the punch line be as delicate as you want it to be. A two-winged ice sculpture. A wrought-iron gate.

Chickenwing

The secret is only good guys want to fight.

I am scared to fight. I'm not afraid of taking a punch. I do not fear getting dragged to the ground. Rather, I am scared of the repercussions, of how each fist will echo for years. In grade school, I took my fair share of abuse because I did not want to get in trouble with authority—the gym teacher in bright blue basketball shorts, the bus driver with the handlebar moustache, the vice principal with the jet-black hair.

To be called a chicken is the worst insult in the world of wrestling—it is enough to cause a blood rival to lose his cool and attack with malice, enough to coax even the biggest coward into throwing a punch. To be reluctant to fight is common in this world—it always heightens the drama when a champion tries to duck a challenger, the hero landing a few glancing blows before the villain lands a cheap shot and sneaks up the ramp, clutching his title to his chest.

The first time I caught one of my tormentors with a knee and bloodied his chin, I was more concerned with getting caught, being dragged out of the lunch line and ridiculed as a brown-haired boy with a spiked haircut spit blood into a paper towel. When he fell, I froze. I looked around for the inevitable swooping in—the crackle of a walkie-talkie, my potato-chip lunch crushed.

It never came.

Law enforcement primarily uses the chickenwing to subdue; it is part of the use-of-force-continuum standard. This is called pain compliance—its purpose is to direct the actions of the subject. It is implied that when the subject complies, the pain will be lessened. Arms behind your back. Stop struggling. Stop struggling.

To this day, I don't know how I got away with it. I have dreams where I am made to pay for what I did: I somehow killed the kid—I never stopped even after the bell rang; I continued to pummel away until I knocked the life out of him.

There are moments in wrestling where the hero can fight too much—law enforcement officers come down in nondescript polo shirts and attempt to take the house-of-fire babyface into custody and, in a moment of rage, get hip-tossed and thrown out of the ring, before being subdued by sheer volume and dragged out of the arena, their hands tied behind their backs.

When they come for me, I will tell them I cannot put my right arm behind my back. I will be given the benefit of the doubt because of the color of my skin and the fact that I am a good guy who just had a little too much fire in him. I will explain that I could not let go, and they will let me go.

John Cena Is the Only Thing
That Is Left Here

You couldn't blame her: the weeks before had thrown trees through places trees have never been, had torn scars through asphalt, had made neighbors pour out from front doors that no longer exist, like children stomping on anthills to watch insects stronger than we'll ever be tangle their bodies together to escape the world they've built as it caves in.

But nothing about the game was real: the way his grotesque mouth would open to nothing, the way those textures didn't deserve mapping. Here is a place that doesn't deserve the shaping of polygons, where we dig with our hands and still say the wrong things at dinner tables, and we suffer despite not knowing what exists outside of cages; the world around us knows more about where we are than we do—we, brooms in hand, bringing whatever we can gather, because gathering is the only thing we can possibly think to do.

In the game, he is more superhuman than he is in real life: a man whose muscles swell out from underneath low-rising socks, a man who can expose skin because he is not worried about the brambles left behind by the wind, a man who can bleed and think nothing of it because there is nothing left to rust. There is no blood. No broken glass from beer bottles or blown-out windows. The weather can cause such false things: there are shapes on maps, there are colored splotches that signify that it is going to rain soon and it will take everything you have.

Instead, we have a version of a man who is a version of a man he has always been, undeviating in anything but his stature—wristbands like the ones he wore on television, a military salute at the beginning of the ramp. He walks in small steps, head always focused on his opponent—as if there is nothing else in the world to focus on except the task at hand. We tend to forget what is happening beyond where we are, a beautiful thing when we are in love, when we are asking for the world's admiration, yet heartbreaking when there are rumors of dead bodies found in the bottom of the lake, a set of bones caught in a basement.

And yet there he was, as inevitable as a news ticker: a statement of a fact, a prayer gone half-answered, the crowd around him moving in patterned unison—they do not deviate from their purpose, arms going up and out and looping until the match is over or the console shuts off.

When I was a child, none of this would've been possible. The re-creation of our heroes would have been too muddled to be taken seriously: a representative on a curved screen; our champion here as a pale blob in blue shorts, nothing differentiating him from the idols of his past or the devils of his present. As a child, I wouldn't have been trusted to cook pots of red beans—I would not have known to let them soak. They would come out hard and bitter, everything would be ruined, and we would all go hungry; everyone would leave this place because there is no weight to hold us down, and we, too, would break pattern into something a bit more believable, going our separate ways until we are the ones at the bottoms of lakes, and instead of being picked up we are driven downward, a cyclone in reverse, a drill downward that places us underneath the dirt with no knowledge of what direction to climb.

And perhaps this is why these days we don't believe in gravity: he takes a leap with a man on his back before sending him crashing to the floor. We beg buttons to try to coax our men to get up because this is what we were taught to do when we were young: taught that there was something we could do if we were down and out on the floor, eyes to the fluorescent lights, that this is our natural reaction, to try to put action into something that has been long left dormant. And so when someone walks in and mistakes what is on the television for something real, despite the fact that this is an artifice of an artifice of an artifice, I cannot fault them: there are dust clouds where houses once stood, and they are dissipating on the wind—we will give directions in regard to where things once were. Despite one's desire to change, to become something new, to reinvent, to wave a hand over a different face, we are still locked in an array of repetition, not of seeing things we can no longer see but of seeing the absence so clearly.

LET ME TELL YOU SOMETHING

Wrestling narratives are repetitive. A challenger
will fight a champion in a nontitle match in order
to obtain a title match. A challenger will pin a
champion in a nontitle tag match to set up a title
match. A champion will pin the challenger in a title
match through nefarious means. The cycle will
repeat. The fight goes on forever.

Front Chancery

The secret is that it's hard to let go.

An unwritten rule is that heroes never give up. When they are in the clutches of a particularly dastardly submission maneuver, they struggle endlessly—they reach fruitlessly outward in hopes of something, anything, to grab on to that would help them reverse the pressure of the hold expertly applied by their opponent, before, inevitably, finding inner strength to power out of the move with one last-gasp effort, as if they've summoned the will of the people chanting their name into some sort of tangible energy, a last breath from an expertly applied chokehold or a momentary break in agony from an awkwardly torqued knee.

On nights where the villain is supposed to look even more villainous, the hero passes out in the hold—a way to demonstrate that the pain was far too great, yet his stubbornness caused him to hold on for just a little bit longer, that he was overwhelmed to the point of exhaustion. The villain holds on a hair too long, as we get a close-up of our hero in peril, face turned the color of pomegranate, before a swarm of referees and men in black emerge from the back curtain to break the hold, making large gestures with their arms as if to say no, the villain eventually letting go and walking backward up the ramp, laughing and smiling the entire way, as the good guy regains consciousness in the ring, befuddled by what just happened.

There are moments when our hero, pushed to his wits' end, holds on to the chokehold a little too long. This is when we know that things are serious—that there is a larger reckoning coming, that something has become deeply personal. The audience forgives this—they know that this is a temporary break, that this is what the villain or the villain's lackeys deserve; a message needs to be sent.

And yet when these things become a pattern, we become disturbed—we're concerned that what was once light will fade to darkness, a look in the eyes that was not there before and hasn't been seen in quite some time.

If the lesson here is that we turn sour by holding on too long, what am I to make of all of this? I still hold moments of violence toward me in my heart that I can regurgitate at a moment's notice: the feel of two textbooks slamming over the back of my head, the soft dull sting of a kick to the stomach.

There are days I think my body is punishing me for all of this: When I see others eat as much as they like but remain thin or when my muscles flare up in odd ways at inopportune times. When I hold stress in my shoulders until it fogs my memory. This, here, is what I am hiding—this is me letting my arms unflex, if only for a moment.

"Stone Cold" Steve Austin
Cannot Be Forgotten

What you want to know is who was my favorite. What you hear is not what you want to hear—a name that means nothing, as it was born from something pressing, a technician with a quick first strike who came of age after you outgrew the lariat, the steel chair. What you want is to hear me say a name that you remember, one that brings up memories of T-shirts and lunch rooms, of catchphrases and gestures. Here is what you remember: the glass-breaking, the beer-chugging, the idea of the everyman telling every boss to go get whipped; what audacity one has to wear a tie when it is so easy to grab it and pull.

What I would like to say is that I remember these things too: black trunks, black boots, everything nondescript—me, if I were asked to fight someone, me, if I were given twenty minutes to get ready. The kick to the stomach, the double over, the chin spiking into a shoulder. The dramatic fling backwards as if springing back from god-knows-what: a flop, and then stillness. What I would like to say is how we all wanted to do this to everyone who told us what to do: coaches asking us to jump higher, a police car slowing to a crawl when approaching a group of kids in dirty jeans walking down a road with no sidewalk.

What power this has over us, what undeniable nostalgia—when he threw up his fists with his knuckles turned outward, we felt that we could do anything, that what we were as men was more than we could ever be as boys, that what ages us can be ignored, that every swift strike was more beautiful than we could remember, that every boot hit flush, that we, too, could put holes in the earth. What a marvel that we can make the world bend around our bodies, what beauty to take the earth with us, caked up around our ankles, as if we are spreading the world thin, as if what is lacking elsewhere can be pressed into our pores until the red clay of the earth dyes our skin rust red.

What I can tell you is that these stories are universal: I remember where I was when the four-wheeled goliath smashed into the side of the ring apron, what I felt when it seemed as if the outstretched leap wouldn't clear the top rope, what happens to necks when hanging upside down, falling backward instead of forward, each vertebra compressed and stacked like a crushed empty can. What I can never tell you is that this is not the past for me: these are bodies that you have left behind, caricatures, with their features bloated, their abdomens distended. I can never tell you what it is like to have the privilege of remembrance—what it is to find past glory lurking in the shadows like a testament—a declaration of something so certain that even the haze of the world can't keep your eyes from squinting to clarity. What went the way of the rattlesnake. What happens after the serpent leaves its pattern in the dirt and fades into the tall grass outside of your apartment, waiting for a drunken night to strike again—to leave welts under eyes and palm prints across cheeks.

What I am about to tell you is true: the man known for being tougher than a two-dollar steak left his wife's bruised body in hotel bathtubs. There was no audience when your favorite memory drove his knee into a woman's back, stunning her, making it to breathe. This is something that you will not remember—this was after your time—this is a man who handed out beatings like the loudest prayer you've ever heard, one that rips through whatever ceiling we have trained our eyes on until the center of our forehead grows warm. What it means to live to tell: to celebrate the illusion of a cracked skull while cheekbones are pressed into carpet. What world this is. What it is like to be 100 percent pure. What the world has come to.

What remains. What the sound of glass is when it is not breaking. What it must be like to interrupt silence with something more than remembrance—what we become when we are alone and left to our own devices. What forgiveness we grant our heroes, and what audacity we give away at the ready when what we consider classic is taken from us. What it is like to not think about these things. What it is like to separate man from action even when these actions are simulacra of actions. What you should know is that the fists are closed, now. What you should know is that when someone is seriously hurt they make an X with their hands; the gloves come out, the cameras pan the crowd. What you are seeing is what you are supposed to see, and what you see you need to believe. Believe me, I know how strange this sounds. Believe that when you hear glass shatter, there are shards somewhere on the floor. Believe that the edges will cut you straight across the scalp. What you remember is a lie. What you love is not what you love. Believe me when I tell you it's worse than you remember. Believe me when I tell you that I know you haven't watched in years.

LET ME TELL YOU SOMETHING

A dead crowd will kill a match. At SummerSlam,
the audience was more interested in a beach ball
than the actual action in the ring. Cesaro, one of the
performers in the match, managed to get his hands
on an overhit serve and tore the latex in half with
his bare hands. The audience booed him out of the
building. There is no desire for anything organic.

Spinning Heel Kick

The secret is the room has been spinning for two weeks.

Not spinning like I am the center pole of a centrifuge, not like how they separate milk from cream, not like my blood in the lab to separate it from itself—red into red, white into white, other colors, certainly, perhaps a gray, perhaps a scarlet, perhaps floating, perhaps clawing at the sides like on a carnival ride, spinning, spinning, perhaps sinking to the bottom. Perhaps purple. Perhaps violet: perhaps separating the n from the word. This is a lot about what it is not, and as of late I am defined by what I am not: I have not had a stroke. I am not dying more than usual, though my body tells me in the middle of the night that I might be: breath vacuuming up through my left side and through my teeth, a shock I can feel in my eyes. I did not mean to use the word "I" here, as I am not detached yet—the room is still spinning, I am still not a lot of things. I could tell you about the tests, but you know the tests. I could tell you about the feeling, but you know the feeling: a couple drinks away from too many drinks, loosened up, ready to kiss the person you've been thinking about kissing, yet too far from kissing the person you've never thought about kissing—darts go where you want them to, cue ball angles are more possible, every song sounds good. Except you know better. Scratch that: except I know better, every bit of me knows better, and this is not better. Let me start again: The room has been spinning for weeks, though it is not spinning, as if you are dreaming about a house that you once lived in. It is your house but it is not your house—the kitchen is to the right, the stairs lead to a different room, the walls change to reveal faces of people you have never considered thinking about: the girl who hands you a lemonade and says my pleasure, hands you a receipt and says my pleasure, who reminds you at that moment of your time in Belgium, where any time you are handed anything they say if you please, not in your language, but in theirs, all strung together—just say "allsyoubelieve" as fast as possible—unless they see your eyes and see your sneakers and sense your stutter and amazement at flavors of potato chips and find that words they find normal you find strange, and then, but only then, they say please: a loss of formalities, of regality, just please. This is what the nurse said to you while you were there, that lovely nurse who would wake you in the middle of the night to take your blood, all the while saying please before sticking the needle through your skin. And maybe that is why the girl who handed you the lemonade is there, because she says my pleasure as charmfully lifeless as someone taking blood, and your left arm hurts from where the needle went in. You forget words but keep talking as if you are not forgetting them: substituting the name of one person for the name of another despite knowing them as two things with two different lives, despite not talking to one of them for years, despite attending the funeral of the other. All the while, the room gently spins, or it doesn't. This is not what I wanted to tell you about. What I wanted to tell you about was when they tried to spin the room back the other way: They told me to close my eyes and they blew hot air into my ears. The nurse said she would wait a minute and then take it out, and I thought she meant the air, that it would be in there until she brought forth a device I have never seen nor ever would see—keep your eyes closed—that would take everything back. Now is the time to tell you that when someone whispers in my ear I see colors: purple, violet. When the bar where we drink gets too loud, and it always does, you talk loudly into my ear so that I might hear what you are trying to say: a drink, another drink, how loud it is. Sometimes I see things there too, but only sometimes. This was more like that: the darkness of my eyes while my lip curled up, folding my nose into my cheek, like I am bracing myself for the air to form words that I want to hear—this is normal, you are going to be okay, there is love here—and yet it never does. It is dark and this might be a love story. This might be a love story because it is romantic not knowing what is killing you: we all love a good mystery. This is the first time my body has a secret admirer and it cannot wait to gossip. The body loves to whisper. I imagine the air filling every crevice of my brain, my spectacular brain that says with a wink that nothing is wrong, all of its wrinkles gathering speed like they are drifting off the dunes—passwords achildhoodnamemisspelled and song lyrics slowmotionisbetterthannomotion and people I have yet to forgive cannotsaytheirnameseven and how to say thank you justsaycrackofdawnasfastaspossible—and yet all I am doing is wondering how to tell you about it. I could say they did a test where they told me to close my eyes, then blew hot air in my ears and then had me open my eyes and recite lists of things in alphabetical order: name something in the supermarket that starts with the letter *A*, and I said apple. *B*, I said banana. Cereal, Doritos, eggs, fish, garbage, no, I meant garbage bags, but you are already on *H* and I have not thought this far ahead. It is time to feel dizzy and close my eyes and get told to keep them open, but I cannot think of *H* with my eyes open—I am seeing the supermarket like

I am seeing my house in the dream: green walls, produce toward the back, and now I am seeing my house that is not my house. House, house, house, if I could remember the house I could remember everything, walking through it and seeing the hot dogs on the plate in the kitchen, the ice cream in the freezer, the juice on the counter. The nurse says the answer does not matter, but God dammit, it does. I could tell you this, but I can't make you feel it and I can't make you be there. I could tell you all of this, but I cannot tell you what comes next, though you can certainly guess: the hot air pours into my other ear and I am asked to recite names this time. *A* is for Adam. *B* is for Brian—of course the answers matter. When we get to the letter your name starts with, the room is spinning as badly as it ever has. When we get to the letter your name starts with, your name is the only one I can think of, but I refuse to say it out loud.

A Giant Is Always Interrupting

The Giant Singh Becomes the Great Khali

A giant is not inherently great, and this is something I learned the hard way. You are taller than the lion you awaken—larger than the sum of the people they make you represent. I cannot imagine your life before this, how everywhere you are draws a crowd, how you tower over the world like a lightning rod in a city of cardboard roofs—we sing your body electric, we laugh as you sing with us. All men first described as great become jokes when the knees start to give out—look how slow you move, look how you stoop only to take a foot to your chest from someone smaller. A giant without humanity exists only to bend to the wills of men; we believe that all those who see beyond trees into deserts need humility—that no matter how many times you are chopped to the ground, it is justifiable. To kick you while you are down is as welcome as tea on a cold afternoon. You and your frame are standing in the way of a lesson to be learned: How dare you come forth with anything but grace in your giant hands? You, giant, are conquered. Please, go in peace until we evoke your name for the next great unlearning.

Figure-Four Armlock

The secret is that in wrestling, everything you do comes back to you.

When people ask me how I got into watching professional wrestling, I find it difficult to pinpoint an exact moment. My mother worked as a librarian, so most of my days after school were spent at the library, doing schoolwork, drawing comics on copy paper, and reading paperbacks underneath crafting tables. Some days, I would go play with a friend of mine from school whose family lived across the street. He had an extensive collection of wrestling action figures: Hulk Hogan, Jake the Snake, Ricky "The Dragon" Steamboat. When we would play with them, I was given the wrestlers, while he and his brother claimed the much more decadent action figures: the ones with multiple points of articulation, who could hold giant bazookas, who could shoot small projectiles a few inches into the air. Wrestlers without connotation are simply men, their muscles molded in plastic, their hair stiff. I did not know about Hogan's extensive title reigns, about Steamboat's ability to effortlessly climb to the top of any structure.

I have a continued interest in what I am made of—how thick my neck is, how much fat I carry with me through the world. I weigh myself every day except for Sunday. I put on swim caps and compression gear and sit in a small white egg, which somehow, miraculously, tells me how much muscle I have gained or lost. It is not enough to simply be.

Recently, I participated in a 3-D scan in order to find out the composition and measurements of my body. In the scan, I was asked to take off all my clothes and stand on a small rotating platform. As I spun, unseen cameras took multiple photos of me, naked and spinning. At the end of the scan, a small gray avatar of me popped up on my phone. It was unmistakably me: how my right shoulder sits considerably lower than my left, how my stomach hangs over my waist, the roundness of my head, the shape of my nose. There were statistics about how much body fat and lean muscle I carry, although it was hard to believe these things beyond the rotating image of my body—how smooth it looked, despite all my blemishes, the red bumps on my skin grayed out to flatness.

Currently, they use similar technology to make WWE action figures. While there isn't nearly as large of a market for these collectibles these days, there is still some sort of nostalgia attached to them. There are plenty of backstage videos of newly anointed superstars talking excitedly about their first-ever WWE action figure. There are artists who create their own figurines for wrestlers who have yet to be action-figure worthy or who feel as if the customization of their characters is not extensive enough. The wrestlers do their signature poses as cameras rotate around them taking hundreds of thousands of photographs to create a 3-D model that can then be printed and colored.

On one particular playdate, I was once again given a wrestler to play with—nondescript with his wrestling trunks and lack of movement from the waist down. But I could raise his arms and turn his head from left to right. In a death-defying act, I sent the figurine off the top of the stairs to crash on the landing below—if only for a moment, he could do something superhuman. On landing, one of his arms completely separated from the shoulder, a plastic socket, leaving a round hole where the doll's shoulder had once been.

I attempted to jam the broken arm back into its shoulder, although my fingers kept slipping, the plastic cutting my fingertips and digging into my nail bed. I promised that I could fix it, although I kept failing—I simply didn't have the strength. Despite the complete lack of regard for the wrestling figurine leading up to this point, my classmate and his brother were apoplectic. There had to be some sort of penance, some sort of hell to pay for destroying something so delicate. In wrestling, there is something called a receipt: if a wrestler messes up and injures a wrestler for real, that wrestler expects to receive something in return: a stiffer slap, a harder wrench. There are times when the falseness becomes real—the time for pretend is always being blurred. My receipt came in the form of an arm for an arm: they grabbed my hand and tried to rip my arm from its socket, pulling as hard as they could to see if they could somehow tear my body away from itself, pinning me to the ground and grabbing at my wrist like it was a shovel stuck in concrete. I did not dare fight back—I would like to say it was because I deserved it, but "deserve" has nothing to do with anything. I wanted to see if they could do it—if my body would allow it, to see just what it is I am made of.

CM Punk's Return Is Imminent

A name synonymous with the fact that we do not like what we are shown, that we have paid good blood to see something different than whatever it is we expected. The true joy in this game is found in predictability—in all things, we want to feel smarter than everyone else by being able to predict the patterns. There is no way a simple punch would put the champion down for the count; it would require something with more glitz and pageantry—a flying elbow to the heart, a knee to the face. We know that all of these moves are transitional—a buildup to something monumental; a stopgap on our trip west; the idea that whatever we do is never permanent, that there is perpetually something more waiting for us in the future. For you, it was after lying in the corner while the story was elsewhere: the piece of modern art in the corner mistaken for misplaced metal, the struggle against a lightly placed bottom of a boot that looks to wear you down instead of giving you an opportunity to catch your breath.

We forget the things we promise to never forget much faster than we ever anticipate. I can't remember the gaps in moments the same way anymore, the moment you changed the sequence from a bulldog to a lariat, or even what it meant at the time—somewhere in between good and evil we change the pattern. All we know is that you are gone and you may never return, though we bask in your imminence—a savior that is always on the precipice of returning, a silence cut to static, a return unspoiled.

Centuries after you left, the trick was revealed—before you ascended to a different plane, you said you would return within a generation, though much like when we chant your name we mean something entirely different than the words, there are things that are open to gaps in translation: epiphanies and appearances, arrivals and presence. You knew this too: That there was time for a man to be lawless because that is what is appreciated here, in a place where hell exists underneath the floorboards and can be assembled with open-weave steel mesh. That we can peer into the linear divide through the chain link. That the only way out is to break down the cage until both feet hit the floor. These arms that climb through the cutout holes in the side netting are too short to box with God, as if God would ever fight fair—our king of equivocation, of saying we can live forever if we lie in a dark room with a cracked skull until we bleed out.

Instead, you have ascended and we are still here—I am still here. Most days I am able to live my life without thinking of the eternalness of being awake; I cannot feel what it is to be alive, because I simply am. I cannot fathom what it is like to have you return, though I imagine it multiple times—a great bursting forward, a lightning strike. There are debates as to whether it will be sudden or gradual, as if we can feel you all around us as we chant your name over and over like an incantation—as if we can summon anything with our words, the same way we open ancient doors or bring back some version of the dead in mirrors. The word is truth, and the word is you, even though our mouths crack and salt over because the spoons are too long and we are alone.

If you are who you say you are, you are everything: Every

back of a head we mistake for someone we loved once, every quarter we see on the sidewalk only to realize that it is a piece of chewing gum turned black from the sun. The snakes I see when I close my eyes. The halo. The apparitions don't have to be what we believe them to be: long hair lost in an unmasking, tired eyes found in the wood grain of a library door. The best imitations of you all lack conviction, while the worst are filled with passionate intensity: chanting your name over and over until we can somehow turn the contents of our collector's cups into something more sparkling than water, your forgotten wife into you, men who move too slowly to escape a vise into you, all of us into you, into you, into you, into you, into you, into you, into you.

LET ME TELL YOU SOMETHING

Sometimes it is goddamn magical. Kofi Kingston, the longest-tenured Black wrestler in WWE, was a last-minute replacement for another injured superstar in a six-man elimination match. Kofi, a reliable performer who never had a heavyweight championship opportunity in eleven years, went the distance in a loss. His performance built a movement to get Kofi into the main event of WrestleMania—the company had the wherewithal to throw obstacle after obstacle in his path, mirroring his experience as a Black performer in WWE but finally culminating in a dramatic tear-filled victory. In his postvictory promo, when asked about his championship journey, he stated, "You don't know if the hard work is going to pay off. It's paid off right now."

Arm Bar

The secret is the wrestlers know you know.

The phrase "technical wrestler" doesn't have a set definition. It is usually applied to wrestlers who try their best to be realistic in the ring: focusing on moves and holds that appear like they would legitimately cause damage rather than attempting to wow the crowd with aerial maneuvers. They utilize techniques that look as if they could legitimately be used in a fight—embracing grapples and strikes. The phrase is also regarded as a pejorative in wrestling circles: most technical wrestlers are devoid of charisma. Making offense look realistic is less important than the showmanship of the whole endeavor.

When Dean Malenko was in his early wrestling career, he was given the moniker "The Shooter," mostly due to his resemblance to Royce Gracie, the Brazilian jiujitsu superstar. A "shoot" in professional wrestling is something unscripted: an accidental elbow to the face, an on-screen rant that gets a little too personal, or a technical difficulty. In Malenko's case, the bookers wished to give the appearance that he was a legitimate fighter with an extensive catch-wrestling and MMA background—a legitimate tough guy who could take anyone out in a "real" fight and thus had a distinct advantage in a professional wrestling ring. Malenko had grown up in the wrestling business but had no such amateur background in the sport. The idea of Dean Malenko was an illusion of authenticity: someone pretending to be real pretending to be fake.

Malenko was known as "The Man of 1,000 Holds"—meaning he had 1,000 different ways to wear his opponent down into submission. However, when most wrestling fans hear this moniker, their thoughts immediately turn to Chris Jericho, Malenko's blood rival in the late '90s. Jericho had defeated Malenko, causing Malenko to "leave the company" for a considerable amount of time. During Malenko's absence, Jericho would constantly goad him, declaring himself to be a better technical wrestler than Malenko ever was. At the pinnacle of this feud is a promo considered to be one of the greatest of all time: Jericho stood in the ring, scroll in hand, and declared himself to be "The Man of 1,004 Holds." He then began to list every single one—arm drag, arm bar, the Moss-Covered Three-Handled Family Gradunza, arm bar, the Saskatchewan Spinning Nerve Hold, arm bar, the Shooting Star Staple Superpress—before the show cut to commercial. When the show returned, Jericho was on hold number 712: arm bar. Even after this promo, Malenko didn't return until two months later to exact his revenge, disguising himself as a *luchador*, winning a battle royal, and eventually taking out Jericho and winning his title.

Malenko's mystique was created in his absence: an over-the-top wrestling personality was the one who did the heavy lifting. When Malenko unmasked, it was easily one of the greatest crowd reactions of his career, despite the fact that Malenko had done little to nothing in the interim. His greatest story was told by his greatest adversary.

Even among friends, conversations turn toward violence. After a few drinks, we all swap war stories: How many fights have you been in? For me, the answer is endless—I've taken my fair share of punches, of kicks to the stomach. I've been slapped and shoved. Pushed up against lockers until they stop rattling. But in my mind, those don't count, and in most people's eyes they don't count either: they want to know about fists thrown, one-on-one contests, brawls pulled apart. Those are the ones that are legitimate. Those are the ones with a good story: of being pushed too far, of taking a hockey stick across the wrist before pressing a kid up against a retractable bleacher, of him shaking his hair out of his eyes before I drove the back of his head into the lacquered wood of the risers.

I wonder if I am the one to tell you about the fights my body has seen: With the exception of a few fingers, I have never broken a bone. All of my black eyes were inadvertent. I have never climbed inside the squared circle or the octagon. With a few exceptions, these fights were meant to be playful—simply for fun. The second I took it seriously it would start to hurt, I told myself. If I took it seriously, the mystique would disappear.

Brock Lesnar and the Woman I Am About to Marry Are Both Billed from Minneapolis–St. Paul, Minnesota

She, just across the river, in a house her father bought, with a square key she keeps in a watering can when she goes running by a high school she always rolled her eyes at, a steep climb to the octagon-shaped water tower, each side made of Kasota stone and brick. It's a different place in the summer, I hear—there are different tires to be put on the car when the chunks of ice in the river shrink to the size of mangoes; they are kept in a clumsy pile on the front porch until it is warm enough to get wherever it is we are going.

I was here once, without you, in the way that you can be without someone you always knew—in the way of bridges; of how I walked across the river before I drove across it, finding myself going the wrong way in a car we will later take to the shore's end; of existing in a world I do not belong in just yet; of having arrived before my time.

He, a monolith of a body, human in the same way that we categorize things that we do not know but wish to get close to: a chest pink, a nose broken. There is a tattoo that stretches from the navel to the throat of a sword, and you and I know that all things here are metaphor; some bombastic gesture toward a world we have never seen; something magical and hierarchical; something more royal than the blue of your dress, the blue of my eyes.

You do not watch these battles with me and I understand: you, underneath a barrier of blankets, me, wasting my time to see what the end result is of a thing that does not carry any weight beyond the realm in which it exists. We live in a world where none of this matters: we drive across rivers to buy groceries—a carton of eggs, bananas in bunches.

This whole thing is an illusion and this is what I struggle with—that I live in a world where the lie is larger than any flexed bicep, than any shoulder rounded toward the camera to show just how serious this threat might be. The world in which I love you is shared with the suspension of belief: how grown men can jump into the arms of others, how when we flip head over heels we somehow manage to graze a shoulder before tumbling toward the earth.

There are rivers here, too, where we have made our home: where the world splits into something we regard as duality even though it is just a space where the water has rushed enough to erode the stones to slickness—a divide that gives us pause. The world is unmarked as if we believe there are beasts there, dragons, maybe, all bubbling up, wingless and tongue scorched as if they are from a world that we have not yet imagined.

In the world where all of this is real, the x is dropped: we do not pronounce anything more than what we are expected to, and the letter whistles through our teeth as we leave our tongues dormant. Instead, we shape words in ways foreign to these mouths—I find myself saying words the way that you have always said them, in homes with square keys: bag, man, asparagus.

He, he exists in a world with which we are unfamiliar—one

of narratives and advocates, of throwing his fists toward the ground as fireworks shoot toward the sky. He lives, though, in our space, a space of thousands of lakes, of a sharp knee to the gut that causes men larger than me to double over, of cauliflower ear, of other words I shape in new ways since our whirs find their way to the same frequency.

This is fiction: one of the first lessons we learn is that the punches are never real—they are as open-fisted as a magnolia, fingers disappearing into something that looks like air. And yet here is something that is true: the man we call the beast incarnate, the one, the alpha, the conqueror of worlds we are unfamiliar with—he is as real as we imagine him to be. He makes sandwiches for his sons. He takes them hunting in the woods behind the woods. In the world where blood does not turn black and white, he fights out of elsewhere—a rural town where he has moved his family, a quiet place we mispronounce, a place not found on a map unless you know where to look. A house with three sets of doors. A window that faces the sun.

You are from a city that could have been named after a pig's eye but instead was named after a saint I learned about in a church in a town named after bridges—the water snaked in such a way that one bridge was never enough to keep us floating. Where we are from is who we are and where we will return.

Everywhere he is, a new city. A new courthouse, a new water tower, built on the ability to take another man and lift him off the ground, up and over his head—to send others into an onyx oblivion, a smoothed stone, a catch and release. Every town has the same name. Every city a heart. Every street sign a way out.

Enough about where we are from. Let me tell you about the place where we are fighting out of. Let me tell you of its rivers—of how our porch swarms with black cats and tree leaves; of how divided it all must seem to anyone; of how it was broken by straight-line winds and tornadoes; of how we somehow managed to stir our wings before we were left for dead. This is our home and we will fight until the death of it. This is where we lock doors, where we cut bell peppers. This is a place where we can catch an elbow and shake it off like it was a short-haired shout from a rooftop. Break the arms of the other cities. Hold their faces to their grass. This is where we build our argument—where we make our stand, where we build the concept of forever even though it seems so in-finite, where it spreads further than a knife blade, where we ask ourselves what it means to be crowned. Let me tell you about where we are from. Let all of this happen before the bell rings. Let us fill this space with our elbows. Watch how we fight out of. This is a city I will never know without you.

Mr. Perfect Alone in a Room
Where He Will Die

The secret, of course, is that he wasn't.

A quick strike to the head followed by something twisted and aerial would put him out, eyes glazed over, unblinking toward the ceiling. He lost almost as many times as he won—catching an elbow to the chest or to the crown of his square-blocked head, his shoulder bouncing off the mat at an odd angle: obtuse or acute, certainly never perfect. The thing that tried to put you away shared his name, yet it was also flawed: elegant in its float over, its setup, the cruxes, elbows, and knees locked together, the soft spots exposed. It was beautiful and then it wasn't—for something to be perfect, something should be guaranteed, and it wasn't. A kickout before pinfall, a stunned crowd prepared to chant "three" as if it were a proclamation, something so sure and steadfast that it exists on a horizon like no one has ever seen: a declarative statement of nature and God—three as I am, three as the Great I Am, a sun disappearing into the waters of every lake at once.

And yet this is what was supposed to happen. What is not perfect is beautiful in its struggle—here is a man who can do anything, a man who can toss a basketball over his right shoulder and whisper it home, who can amaze heroes of worlds where such a thing as chance exists, where luck determines an outcome. And still, he never won the big one: he never put the giants to sleep, he never had the man out cold even though that is what should be given unto him: the three, the thing to hold on to, the extra weight that comes with being divine.

Here's something you already knew: the perfect one is dead, crushed by the weight of his own heat, a pocket of air where blood should be, a hiccup, an imperfection. What made the man perfect was not what he did but what was done to him: snapping hair back after every near miss, doubling over like he was kicked in the gut when he was only almost kicked in the gut. Believe that his leg had been deadened, believe that the chop caught him flush. Believe all of these things so you can believe the narrative, flawless in his execution. Believe that he is dead, that people die in hotel rooms all the time, that someone always has a key and a fresh pair of sheets. That when you enter a room, no one has ever lived here but you.

There are nights when I forget if it is better to be perfect or better to be beautiful. If there is a difference between expertly playing a man stronger than iron or playing dead. You know these things, of course; you know them because you are perfect. You know that you have attained your purpose, that you are complete and that I am too—I am complete in my failure, in my ability to make all things beautiful in comparison—that you can be amazed at how poor perfect can be, that I will drop the ball when it is thrown to me: it will skip over my taped knuckles and spiral aimlessly to the cold ground. It will be declared perfect: it will be as it should be, me, trying to pull my finger from its socket, trying to grasp harder than I have ever grasped before. I am not faking this:

believe me when I tell you I need ice, believe me when I say I wish I could go on.

There are bears where we are both from—they emerge from the timber like the rattle of a slow drum. Play dead, our parents would tell us, let them sweep over you, let them smell your hair, the spearmint in the chewing gum you have let drop from the corner of your mouth. When I have a son I will tell him these things too—that it is okay to be beautiful, that it is okay to lose like no one has ever lost before. I will walk with a limp when it is necessary, I will call my shots from the baseline. I will be remembered for something that is the opposite of what I was. I will lose and the bears will wash over me like I was never there.

In Which I Imagine Running into Shinsuke Nakamura at Waffle House One Night

Mostly so I can teach him about how this whole thing works, although he knows—the parking lot is vacant most nights around this time of night; the air is cold, the floor slick. I could tell him about how I fell in love after midnight, how separation is key here: white from yolk, cream from coffee, each square a pit to fall into, rounded on some edges, hard and harsh like the prongs of a fork on others. The lights flicker and pulse, and the scraping of metal on metal is a comfort of sorts; if they were to let us behind the counter we could pretend that we were in my kitchen fishing for spatulas.

We should never be awake at this time of night, at this time of morning—lights have already gone out, we are looked at through tired eyes, dried out from smoke or from sleeping with contact lenses in so we could see each other in the dark instead of seeing only shadows of hands, the swift movement of hair. I could tell him that this ended at the bottom of a cup or a song on a jukebox or when the woman at the cash register punched the yellow ticket through its heart, but we all know the sun is coming up or the day is starting and this is an aubade of sorts. A parting of lovers? No, that word is reserved for dinners with wine and desserts after—the curve of a spoon, a tablecloth, something that cannot be wiped away with a dirty rag wet with soap.

Instead, this is another night that should mean nothing, but it never does. I could tell him how we didn't have kitchens like this where I grew up, and he would nod in the same. I have never been to Japan, but I can imagine what it does not have the same way I can choose to not know things: secret intentions, how everything is going to end. I could tell him that there are seven neon-lit sanctuaries within miles of my new house; that a person I loved loved its namesake (or did he?)—how evenly the butter spread until everything was caked over. We cover. We chop.

But mostly, I could tell him about the persistence of it all: how when your town is destroyed and you come out from hiding underneath a mattress, the griddle will be on even if the jukebox doesn't play anything but sirens and the selling of the belief that it is truly worse than it looks, and believe me, it's bad. Shinsuke, I don't know what Waffle Houses you've been to, but I hope you've been to the one my cousin loved, just over the Maryland border. I hope you've been to the one where my father and I stopped, my car still filled with an old desk and a half-broken television. The one where I took the woman I love on a first date, where we went on our anniversary but haven't returned to since. My cousin hasn't been to a Waffle House in years—I hope they have mouths where he lives, but I can never be sure. I shouldn't be talking to you about these things so late in the evening. It is late, too late for coffee, and I am tired.

Instead, take this with you: These places we are from, they are always. They persist. They are always around us, even on the days we don't always notice.

PART THREE

SURELY
THIS IS IT

Eye Rake

The secret is if you see something, you're supposed to see it.

If they linger too long on a wrestler who is injured, it is for the purpose of narrative and is a part of the story; if the camera quickly cuts away and does everything to prevent showing the blood, chances are things did not go as planned. Before every television taping there are "dark matches," which are contests not meant to be seen by anyone but those in the audience. Typically, these matches are meant to hype up the crowd and prepare them for the show that is about to start—the local DJ playing the hits before the headliner starts their set. Here, wrestlers try things out that are not ready to become canon: new moves, the first draft of a new character. Often these matches serve as tryouts for wrestlers, entertainers who have caught the eye of WWE and whom WWE is hoping to bring up to the main stage. It is here, in these gaps, that the true stories are told: before a story is ready to be seen, it exists on a level that is both tremendously human and somewhat ghostly—even the phrase "dark match" seems to carry an ominous weight, as if it somehow shouldn't exist, as if it should be erased from any and all memory.

I think of my body in these terms: how there are things that should never be seen, how I still pause any time I need to take my shirt off with the knowledge that someone else might see me, how I crop the lower half of my body in every photo in hopes that a stranger will not notice that it is not there. There are moments where I believe my body looks strong and powerful, yet I find myself constantly tugging at the edges of shirts, wondering how exactly I move through the world.

My wife likes to make fun of the fact that I am always sitting in the dark—she comes home after a long day and I am straining to read things on my laptop or squinting at my phone. It is something that I don't think about—I am not overly concerned about where light comes from or when the sun is going to fall to a level where it streams in through the top half of a French door. I consider myself bright—I do not hide from spotlights. I love how my voice carries across a room in a way that makes people want to pay attention—authoritative and dulcet as a ring announcer breaking through the crowd to announce a winner by disqualification. But there are many moments where I find myself not ready—green as a gooseberry, undeserving of entering any type of story, my stomach too round, my shoulders too pale.

I am letting you know all of this, but I am not letting you see this. In the wrestling industry there's something called a dirt sheet—undisclosed information about a show and the ways the night is going to go: what marks each wrestler needs to hit, the talking points of the announcers, the winner of each of the matches that are never seen. The dirt sheets talk about redos and retapings, about errors made in production, about entrance music blared too loud. They are somewhere between darkness and light—a red clay that is forgotten about until it turns a sole of a shoe from a bright white to a light orange.

So consider this my confession, an admission that it is impossible for me to exist in two worlds at once, despite wishing I could somehow compartmentalize my obsession with a faux sporting event that has left men broken and burned out, that has celebrated everything I try separate myself from. There are things that are simply too large to not be a part of—their blackness will swallow you whole if you allow it. Even when we wish for things to not be seen, they are witnessed anyway—the inadvertent kick to the eye, the broken nose. They draw you back into the universe filled with the strangest things that make you question what you love. I am here for this. It is dark, but I am here.

Chris Jericho and How the World Ends

The beauty of this is that we saw it coming, waking up in the morning to reports that the other side of the world has gone black—that the future is here but we can only see where it is not, cloaked in the past, all of the lights out. This is worse than we could ever imagine: we imagine glamour, panic in the streets, our neighbors huddled together after my father cuts down the dead apple tree in the front yard (it has since blown down in a storm) and sets it on fire to warm our hands. It is the future now: houses that we have not yet lived in, places that we have never been to—we announce our arrival shining like a mirror ball, we reflect any light that is left. There will be testimonies: shouts of never, of how there are a thousand and one ways to hurt you, and I will list them here. The first is to crush your head with my knee. The second is to arch your back until your ribs stretch out like gates rusted in the rain. The third is to crack your skull against my shin—to turn myself into a table that jumps up to meet you: a table with no bread or wine or God or salt. I will spare you the others, but I will tell you a story. Where I am from, we eat twelve grapes at midnight—sometimes green, sometimes purple. I used to shove them all into my mouth and chew: the acid of the skins sticking to my tongue, the coldness sneaking into my nostrils. It was for good luck for the year ahead, my grandmother would say, as if luck had anything to do with any of this, although it is dark and you are cold like the pulp of grapes. The key is to eat them one at a time: to be patient, to count the threes the fours the fives before the clock strikes again, to know that it is time for us to ignore the lions at the gate. Are you not dazzled? Are you not impressed with how the seconds get crushed to sweetness? Today, the numbers reset to zeroes, no code to break, no cipher, nothing more than the cascading of nothing larger than one—the end of glamour, the end of the world as we know it. Today, we chew in the dark and do not swallow: this is the end of grapes, no one will take the time to harvest them, to pluck them from branches in bunches and slip them into plastic bags with holes in them—presumably to help them breathe. Tomorrow, stores will be empty: heels of bread facedown in dark aisles, jars of jelly smashed open. The walls of this city will not hold us safely: if these walls could talk, they would say nothing before they turned to fragments. Hope resides in a return: to normalcy, to simple transactions at diners, to a white light that will save us from rawness.

And then the lights flicker, downrushing this house with something we thought we would never see again, our grief disappearing with the glow.

And then nervous laughter, a kiss on the cheek, the swallowing of pulp, the decision to stay awake or to sleep dictated by the banging of pots and pans outside.

Later, I whisper to you. Later, after we shut the door and turn off the lights, I whisper that when the world ends I do not want to be here—I want you to lose me to the earth earlier than the earth is lost. Here is something you should never think about: Do not think about our children, and the color of their eyes. Do not think of their end, their children's end. Do not think of them pushing buttons in their sleek cars in garages we will never see. Do not picture them inhaling the smoke until they are sprawled on the floor. Do not imagine the world without them. Do not picture the world continuing, their blood and our blood tamed by the rising end.

LET ME TELL YOU SOMETHING

Like in all fiction, there is a denouement. A classic match has a sequence that leads up to the end: a massive top-rope maneuver that leaves both competitors down and exhausted, or a moment where each wrestler absorbs the other's second-best shot yet still leaves room for a comeback. The crowd can sense the end could come at any moment. It could all be over at any time.

Asuka Means Tomorrow

Tomorrow, I'll call someone to see about the overgrown weeds in the backyard. Tomorrow, I'll see if my body will allow me to go for a walk—to drag it across familiar paths I haven't seen in months in hopes that my bones will not collapse in on themselves. Tomorrow, I will dye my hair—some strands purple, some strands pink. Tomorrow, I will call someone I love and forget to tell them that I love them. Tomorrow, I'll be forgiven. Tomorrow, I'll learn a mother language. I'll say every syllable correctly. I will pass these words down. Tomorrow, I'll go out into the desert. I'll start a fire even though it is too hot for flames. I will see a bird. I will touch a lizard. I will build a tent even though I cannot picture my body inside anything that is outside. Tomorrow, I'll drink more water. I'll climb a tree. I'll keep my palms open. I'll find true North. I'll consider going there, tomorrow. Tomorrow, I'll remember to eat. Tomorrow, I'll believe what I say. Tomorrow, a caring and reluctant thank-you. Tomorrow, I'll be undefeated. Tomorrow, I won't forget to do my stretches, the ones they've named after me because there are no other words. I'll name myself after something that never arrives. Tomorrow, I'll find another heaven. Tomorrow, I'll shimmer. I'll wear something colorful, with pieces of silk stitched together in odd places. Tomorrow, I'll be stitched together in odd places. Tomorrow,

I'll mean it. Tomorrow, I'll keep the doors open—let the wind come through the windows and leave like it was never there. Tomorrow, I'll be able to look myself in the mirror. It will be easy, tomorrow. I'll learn how to ice skate. I'll sharpen my blades to the point where they'll have no choice but to glide. I'll find a pond. I'll wait until the water freezes over, transforms into something else entirely. I'll keep my eye on the clock. I'll wait all day. I'll watch the sun go down, watch the sky turn pink, then blue-black. I won't think of how cold it will be. I won't think of falling.

LET ME TELL YOU SOMETHING

We're going home. The referee is typically in contact with production and knows the precise moment to tell the performers that it is time to wrap things up. This sometimes includes what is known as a "false finish"—a series of dramatic events made to trick the audience into thinking the match is going to be over, only for a wrestler to miraculously kick out at 2.9. The false finishes make the real finish seem more real.

Irish Whip

The secret is you can stop at any time.

A lot of fans dislike anything that makes wrestling seem less real, whether that is Kota Ibushi wrestling a blow-up doll, or Fujimoto fighting Tin Tin, a wrestler in a massive giant panda costume. This is called "kayfabe"—the portrayal of the false as true, demonstrating that what happens in the ring, as well as the rivalries and relationships, are not staged or predetermined. When kayfabe is broken, it breaks the illusion of wrestling.

In the Irish Whip, or the hammer throw, a wrestler grabs his opponent's arm and spins, swinging his opponent in the direction of his choosing—into the ropes, into a barricade, or into the corner turnbuckle.

The idea behind this is falser than any feat of strength, any moment where the undead rise again to gain revenge. You cannot move another person in a direction they do not want to go—you cannot make someone run endlessly until they hit a space where they either stop or spring back with an equal amount of force.

How I wish this were real—that someone could grab me by my arm and sling me in whatever direction I want to go, never deviating from my line, never slowing down until I reach my destination, where I will unceremoniously smash into the side of a building, before regaining my wits, recognizing that, once again, I can move on my own. Start fast and end fast.

There are stories of people being hit by stray bullets fired from half a mile away. Near my house, a student was shot and killed in a parking lot in the middle of the day from a gun six blocks away. There are bullets lodged in the sides of stucco buildings—holes in brick. I have never seen a bullet slow to a stop, lose its elevation before slowly spinning harmlessly into the grass below. I don't believe it possible. Where you are going is always where you are going.

I have two fears in this world: One, that my body will stop, unannounced. Something inside of me will break and I will never see it coming. My heart will stop. My lungs will stop. The halting process will begin and end in an instant, and I will be left on a sidewalk somewhere until I am carried away. My other fear is infinity: that I will be set in motion and I will not be able to stop—nightmares of cars moving backward while I jam the brake pedal, images of falling endlessly down a bottomless pit, my body growing old and frail while falling, never thinking that there is an end somewhere. But most I think of outer space—of how once something is set in motion, it can never stop until it hits something, and the tiniest inertia can send you into an endless void, spinning head over feet until the oxygen gets thinner and thinner. That there is nothing that can be done from the inside; that I can't tell my bones to pivot—that no matter how loud my heart might get, it can't change directions; that I will forever be waiting for the ropes to catch me and send me back.

A Giant Is Always Interrupting

Paul, the Apostle, the Giant

They give you a new name when you arrive—something that states something apparent to anyone who will lay eyes on you. Our names could be used for something more: to reveal a secret that would remain hidden in silence. We know your name when things get serious; we cut through the pageantry to something real, you, named after an apostle who believed that his god was going to return in his lifetime—that despite evidence to the contrary, something that has already risen once will rise again, to pull a shoulder up after the second knockout blow. The real story is that the father of the father of the giant died. The day after the funeral, the father of the giant was found not breathing in a hotel bed too small for his body. Later, the lineage was erased: your blood was no longer his blood. Your name was erased too—rising to the top of the cage before evaporating between the iron bars, as if it were all for show.

Chinlock

The secret is to keep breathing.

We expect these bodies to be elite in every sense of the word—that they do not find themselves tired before the end of every match, that they can only double over in exhaustion when the story has concluded, reached a definitive end.

The wrestler Kenny Omega often points to his cardio training; he can stay fresh throughout the course of a match and therefore has a distinct advantage, considering how long and drawn out a fight can be. Some matches are dictated simply by longevity: The sixty-minute iron man match, in which wrestlers try to gain as many falls before the timer buzzes. The two-out-of-three-falls match, in which wrestlers are expected to win twice. But of course, this is all narrative—to which we ascribe Omega's chances to improve as the match rolls on, expecting that he will not be out of breath, whereas his opponents will have used everything they had in the tank just to keep up.

The fans know if a wrestler is "blown up"—meaning that he is gasping for air well before he should be; the fans take it as an affront to the craft, as if to say you should be in better shape than this, as if each extra breath is taking oxygen from another wrestler waiting in the wings who can make it all the way through a match without breaking a sweat beyond the beads that glisten in the arena lights.

I, too, test the limits of my body—I have found joy in long-distance runs, half marathons and marathons. I am impossibly slow, my body moving in ways that still remain very foreign to me. One thing that I pride myself on is my ability to breathe: how I'm able to keep my breaths shallow despite the number of miles that I put on my legs. I play games with myself, in that I try to see how long I can go without breathing through my mouth, forcing air up and in through my nostrils in an attempt to convince myself that what I am doing is not a big deal, that the work is something that I am more than capable of—that this is something I can do without breathing heavily. Of course, this never lasts long—one shift in elevation and I am wheezing, a slight whistle coming from the back of my throat as my heart rate escalates.

I have learned that it is not enough for someone my size to work hard—I have to appear calm at all times. During races, I am often asked if I am doing okay, if I need any assistance. I receive shouts of encouragement from strangers: to get it in, or to keep working—words I imagine are not shouted at those who look the part. It could be a distance I have run 1,000 times, a short recovery run compared to the longer races I am used to doing, and yet the response remains the same, as if I am not capable—as if this act of my body in motion is an impossible feat.

There is a belief that when you lose weight you lose it through sweat—through liquids leaving your body, through a slow trickle down cold skin. Instead, you lose it in your breaths: the heft bonds with the carbon dioxide—every respiration is a proclamation that you are becoming something better and sleeker than you have ever been. This is something that the world has never told me: that when it is time to leave the body, the weight attaches itself to the lightest thing it can find—an expulsion on the air, an imagining of tissue hitching its wagon to an exhale. This is how the body sheds itself from the inside. This is how it understands its place in the world.

On Razor Ramon Entering the Ring
for the First Time and the Last Time

If something happens to this, something is going to happen to you, he said, and he meant it: gold necklaces wet from dunking a head underwater before walking into the crowd, the sound of a car either screeching to a stop or beginning to accelerate into something faster—the pacing of coming or going as mysterious as anything in this world, where all will eventually be revealed. Of course, we know how the film ends, but we forget it to make ourselves feel more luxurious: say hello to the bad guy is not the line, but it is now—our unlikely hero's last stand as the smoke rises from nowhere, red carpet and red walls as bodies cascade down staircases like dropped coins. The way he remembers it must be different: no black-and-white screens turning into lines of snow, a body facedown in a blue pool while blood swims to the surface of a world that no one owns.

We see him walking through a market in a place where he claims he lives—a place more glamorous and spirited than an island of pines, a place where he is allowed to take anything he wants with a swipe of his gold-fingered hand. He bites through the skin of a plum and chews: once, twice. He spits the pulp in our direction—not out of dislike for the fruit, but for emphasis: this is something that he can do and he will do. How impressive it is, to see someone this bad, with this much disdain, take something of value and make it worthless simply because it is in our heart to do so, to love and to leave, to be graceful yet spin in circles, mumbling into the plywood.

If we are to speak of ends cut short, here's something: while waiting for the bus, I would double girls over and flip them up over my head—shoulder blades resting on the back of my head, arms outstretched like a crucifix, like I am carrying the Lord in the form of a 100-pound teenager: one of the poor ones, the ones with the jeans with words and symbols written on the thighs, pictures I wish I could trace with even just a finger, yet this is where all things are lost at that age, with delicateness, with deliberateness. We are all going to fall someday—the most we can hope for is that we fall forward into something beautiful, something lavender.

Of course, I never fall: she slides down my back and lands on her feet until she asks me to do it again—never a fear of falling, never a fear of death by diamonds, never a fear of sending anyone neck first onto the concrete, for I am gentle: I am not a bad guy, and she will never say good morning or good night or any of those things, because there is no time for salutations. She will die on her own without my assistance: death dropping from within. For the first time, I saw pale raised lines where the skin has died, as if someone had erased pigment with a broken pencil, as if we are left with nothing but the ghost of someone chanting your name from the tops of ladders.

This counts, and we are shocked: a misstep, a crooked flight, and a disappearance—none of this was supposed to happen. No one deserves this final image of rage, no one deserves a body bloated as if it were found washed ashore on the river, shaking with nothing, the rattling of cuts. I think of you, flat on the ground before your eyes roll back, and I am sorry—you, with your thin bones, your thin hair, and my fat fingers, you, impossible to pick up from the ground, you, flush with the cement, you, sharper than the day you were lifted, chin to the sky.

LET ME TELL YOU SOMETHING

A wrestler could get legitimately injured, forcing
the competitors to stop the match. Botches
happen, instances where a move is not executed as
planned—a dive where no one catches the highflyer,
only to have them crash the back of their head into
the concrete, or a palm strike that catches a septum.
It is up to those in charge to call an audible—
a referee might decide to throw the entire match
out, or a wrestler will quickly and unceremoniously
pin his opponent in a way that hardly seems
believable. Traditionally, referees make an X with
their arms to let people know that what is happening
is not scripted and there is legitimate concern.
However, fans became privy to this knowledge, so
bookers would have their performers throw the X
up to make fans believe what they are seeing.

Seiken Punch

The secret is it stays with you.

The best way to cause someone to bleed is to bust an eyebrow open—to forcefully punch down on the brow bone to cause the skin to split. There is an abundance of blood vessels in the forehead, so you'll get a good gush—it will mix with sweat, the face covered in a mixture of blood and salt, dripping and leaving pools on the canvas.

This is called a crimson mask, bleeding so much that your face changes, blood getting in the eyes, turning whatever hair's on the wrestler's head red and slick. The bleeding always comes from the head; no one cares about a bloodied elbow or a back scratched open. The forehead bleeds because it knows someone is watching—if we are to bleed it needs to be for something; it has to elevate, to raise the stakes. When we see blood, we know it's meant to be serious; we like to believe that we wouldn't bleed for just anything.

I am fine with blood. I have scratched a scab until it opens, the blood following the lines defined by my shinbone. I've clipped the tops of my fingers off in the shower. I've had my earlobes pulled to the point where the skin cracks. Chafing during long runs that stains my shorts pink. Needles, where I watch my blood fill glass vials—a violent spurt before it becomes routine. I have good veins, I am told. I know to make a fist to speed up the process. Bleeding is an art, like everything else. I do it exceptionally well.

To make oneself bleed in wresting is called blading—most wrestlers hide a razor blade somewhere in their gear, wait until the perfect time, and slice themselves open. Typically, after a particularly stiff-looking punch, a wrestler will double over, holding his face near the away turnbuckle. He removes the razor and slices across his forehead, being careful not to go too deep, where he would cut an artery. Fans refer to the Muta Scale—named after a match between the Great Muta and Hiroshi Hase, where Muta bladed too deep and the blood stained the pale blue canvas, creating the standard by which all bloody matches are measured. Blood became a trademark for wrestlers such as Abdullah the Butcher, who has massive divot-like scars all over his head. There are stories of Abdullah hiding coins and poker chips in the crevices as a party trick.

When I was younger, I was susceptible to bloody noses. The heat from the radiator would dry out my sinuses. I would feel a drip pick up velocity as I rushed to tilt my head back before it stained my white shirt. I wadded up tissues and plugged them in my nostrils in hopes that everything would coagulate—to force a clot that would allow me to breathe a little bit easier. Most days, though, the blood fell to the ground, leaving a splash of red that sprawled like a squashed tick.

I, too, learned a party trick. I learned that if I bled, I could leave class to go sit in the nurse's office. If I bled enough, I would be excused from gym class—I would get a reprieve from having to take my shirt off in front of the other boys; I could sit and read a book in the bleachers instead of doing half sit-ups and shuttle runs. I spent a year learning how to make myself bleed on command—it gets easier the more you do it, as a bloody nose never truly heals if you keep picking at it. I would press my nostrils together. I would scrunch my nose. I would go to the bathroom and blow as hard as I could, continually checking to see if the paper towels were blotted sanguine. I can't stop bleeding, I would say. There must be something in the air, I would say. I imagine that my teachers were in on it—that they knew that I would do anything to avoid a fate I considered worse than being busted open. That they would whisper about it in the teacher's lounge. That they would tell the nurse to look out for the scam. What it is to be identified not by your blood but by the act of bleeding.

These days it is illegal to blade in most professional wrestling. It comes accompanied by a fine and a suspension or even termination of a contract. All blood is accidental—an elbow to the scalp. A punch to the nose not pulled in time. If a wrestler bleeds on camera, the feed changes to black and white, and we can pretend that it is anything else. Motor oil. Chocolate syrup.

I don't get bloody noses much anymore. Part of it is that I moved to a humid climate—the dry air up north is considered to be the main culprit of cracked vessels. But on occasion, I will wake up with a scratchy throat and a pool on my pillow, the red caked and dried on my cheek. I don't know what I was dreaming about. I don't know what scars I was revisiting while I slept.

The Rock Covered Up His Brahma Bull
Tattoo the Same Weekend I Watched
Him in the Film *San Andreas*

And I cannot blame him for it—to acknowledge our past is to recognize that we were someone else once. We are creatures that lose pounds of skin throughout our lives, so who is to say how we regenerate? You lost more skin than most—every knee rubbed raw, each forehead split from the force of aluminum.

I have a fear of always. As a child, I read about bottomless pits and believed that one false step would send me into a spiral of nothing—that I would fall forever, that I would die of old age, perpetually in a state of plummet. This, too, is how I feared death—imagining myself as bone underneath the earth, seeing nothing and hearing only silence.

Later, I learned that there is a difference between being buried alive and being dead. I learned about the off-chance of heaven, and I fell in love with the odds of it all; there is a promise of movement.

Here is a list of the ways in which I wanted to mark my body: sunrise, ship's wheel, race map. My wife has a star and a state on her right leg. Friends boast a Saturn V rocket, a sprig of arugula, seashells, roman numerals, swirls that look like paint that has yet to dry, names we don't dare speak out loud so we let our bodies put them forth into the world for us.

And you, the bull, staring forward as if to invite any and all comers like an open folding chair or a palm outstretched to the lightwork. This is what it must mean to be synonymous, to be forever attached to something, even though the life you lead is not the life you lead. But you and I know that some things are eternal—that the smell of vinegar always brings me back to the kitchen counter that my mother just cleaned, where I shove sugar into my mouth as I draw the horns on your skin in the margins. We know how skin, too, is paper, how we pulp ourselves into something flatter, how we ring ourselves, how we dry out in the open air.

The bull, now, is dead: a skull in its place, its eye hollowed out—the depth of shadow an illusion, as if the body can somehow cave in on itself. The trick of the eye is something you know about—how we watch the raised hand instead of the hand looking to strike, how the camera never stays in one place despite zooming in on a face always in half surprise. The bone is cracked, as if something's value is determined only long after it has died; a change in perspective stays uncovered like a pot of water boiled over. There is no denying its beauty or that we find peace in dried flowers, a boar with an apple in its mouth, the breath taken when something is over—we compartmentalize, nothing without eulogy—the ice sculpture, the this is your life, the shapes we take.

This body has not earned the chance to be beautiful—it is not something that needs to be remembered beyond the fact that I, too, can raise one eyebrow and look at an imaginary hard camera as if to tell the truth. I, too, was told to die, but I couldn't change my name and clothes—I had to leave a world and never come back; I had to exist as a whatever happened, as if I were ever thought of at all.

Instead, give me a chance to be covered: in honey, in pie crust, in a clear tarp so you can see through to where I should be and have always been. Your name is forever your name, no matter how good you are at escaping from helicopters, the blades starting to slow and bend as the world below falls in on itself. That's me, down there, on my front porch, watching the bones of the earth spit toward the surface as if they are being reborn—forgive me in my panic if I believe them to be alive; it is simply the sight of what was left bouncing on the dirt; you can believe anything is real if you look in the right places. That's me, wondering what the difference is between being swallowed and being buried—I know that you don't mean to, the same way I never meant to draw those lines so crooked that the eyes were askew. They're just contours, edges cragged like split streets. Your body knew this before I ever will—there are stories of cattle sensing the wave before I ever lose my footing; of them running toward the center; of lost-pet flyers stapled to telephone poles days before they topple. They will survive without me and think nothing of it, a new name before the old one scabbed over. That's me, waving upward, falling until the cows come home.

LET ME TELL YOU SOMETHING

Every wrestler has a "finisher"—a signature
move that serves as a knockout blow. These moves
become synonymous with the wrestlers who make
them famous: no one calls John Cena's Attitude
Adjustment a standing fireman's carry powerslam.
Children put other children in Sharpshooters
(scorpion holds), and Yes! Locks (omoplata
crossfaces). This is what the audience is here for—
to see Steve Austin plant his boss with the Stone
Cold Stunner or Randy Orton hit an RKO out of
nowhere. There is always an instance where a
wrestler will try to steal another wrestler's finishing
maneuver and use it against him in a match as an
ultimate insult. It is almost never effective: in the
hands of someone else, a Rock Bottom is just a
falling-forward *uranage* slam. The power is in the
naming of the thing.

Calf Crusher

The secret is that the body is constantly at war with itself.

My body is imbalanced. I am someone who is extremely susceptible to muscle tightness, as my muscles and tendons are constantly overworked because of my weight and how I move throughout the world—my body constantly bracing itself for every step. Our bodies do this to protect themselves—muscles stiffen and stabilize in order to prevent a limb from snapping or an ankle from over-rotating, sending the whole apparatus crumbling to the asphalt.

All of our ailments stem from protection: our bodies harden to the point where we become stone, my calf tight to the point where it seems like there are rocks in it that will only separate if I jam a thumb into a pressure point. Only then will the stone twitch and release.

This is our bodies looking out for us. If we somehow remain impenetrable to the outside—the uneven sidewalks, a vengeful classmate clipping the back of a heel—we can become invincible. We will be ready for anything. We will never succumb.

The beauty of the calf crusher is that it is a compression lock: your opponent presses your muscle into your bone, and your body fights itself until the tension becomes too great and the joint gives out.

I appreciate the concern my body has for me—how it refuses to break, how it chooses to go through the world as if it will be attacked at any moment, dragged to the ground and put in a leg scissor by a passing stranger, a faceless face from my past back to finish the job.

But still it does not think of the pain it brings me—to have a leg that cannot stretch properly, that constantly feels as if it is closing in on itself, as if to be closer and closer to my heart.

Daniel Bryan Is Grateful

And I am too—not that either of us has a choice these days. To turn sour is to see the world as something other than rainbows in gasoline and how they shine when the light hits asphalt, or concrete, or whatever it is that we have paved over with.

He is grateful to have had a body for so long that allowed him to dive headfirst into vipers, to send his body feetfirst into the corner, planting two soles on the chest of a temporary villain before crashing neck first into the mat, before raising his hands to the air as we beg him to do it again and again.

I have been trying to learn gratitude. Here is my body, upright for the moment. Here is my house, the walls painted gray, the lights on—the leak from the roof causing the rainwater to slide behind the primer, though the ceiling holds on for another day. I am scared of ladders. I am scared of a lot of things, and I am grateful.

His name is my name, though you wouldn't know it—when you choose to leave the real behind for the illusion, you are given a new name; gone are the days of mystical beings, of monikers too large for humans to hold. No man with a frozen neck can be called dragon. No man can breathe fire on command;, instead, he holds a lighter close to his heart with a mouth full of rubbing alcohol, moving through the spots quickly so it doesn't evaporate on the tongue, leaving nothing but spirit on the air. Me, I've been called names that are larger than what I am. I am expected to be grateful. I am expected to thank every boy that called me an earthquake. You should hear the things I call my body when I am kept up at night. The names I give it. The words I try to take back in the morning.

He eventually takes it back too—a miracle of science, a vision cleared. No, we don't believe this is real. Yes, we are thankful.

When he returns, he tells us to fight for our dreams so that our dreams will fight for us. Before you dive to the outside again, let me tell you about my dreams. There is the one where I am back in my childhood home, the one with the cream vinyl and the blue shutters and the violet garden in the back. A bird has never kept a space for longer than a season, so who am I to think that I could keep the walls painted, a bed without a headboard? I've slept dozens of places since. I've thought about wings more than once. Here, now, I am telling you about the quails that would escape the lodge down the road—a place where men literally couldn't buy a good look and a solid shot. I dream of their plumes bobbing in the embankments, looking for a place where the ground is just soft enough. It is beautiful. These dreams will never wrap their wrists for whatever I have in my heart. The bell will never sound.

I have come to address you one last time. I am standing in plain clothes in front of my hometown—they have built an arena here just for me, just down the road from the old train station. It is filled with people wearing my face on their shirts, all of my names on their backs. I am grateful. I talk about what they have found in my body. I tell you that I love you. I speak aloud my name. I tell you to remember the dragons. I tell you that tomorrow I will wake up. Tomorrow, I will still be here. Tomorrow, I will live a life where I am no longer wrestling.

LET ME TELL YOU SOMETHING

Most matches, Kenta Kobashi would finish
his opponents with devastating simplicity. A
straightforward lariat or a moonsault off the top
rope. However, he was known as a wrestling
innovator, often taking two separate moves and
combining them into one. He is the inventor of the
Orange Crush, a vertical suplex that transitions into
a powerbomb. He is most known for the Burning
Hammer: an inverted Death Valley driver, in which
he would place his opponent faceup across his
shoulders, before dropping him sideways directly on
his head and neck. It is a move that must be taken
with extreme precision by his opponents, lest they
break their necks. The move is legendary—Kobashi
would only use the move when absolutely necessary.
In total, he used the Burning Hammer only seven
times throughout his entire career. You want to
kill your opponent, but you don't want to kill your
opponent. No wrestler ever kicked out.

A Giant Is Always Interrupting

*The Eighth Wonder of the World Visits
the First Wonder of the World*

Except he can't—there are stories about how he can't squeeze onto buses, how doctors can't put him to sleep, sprawled out on an operating table, vertebrae rubbed smooth as a monolith. Where he grew up, mountains—pyramids, great in their own world, but not made by hands: it is a human marvel to make things hollow. Do not ask me about the scale of these things: the horizon plays tricks if you stare. They, too, cut me open and changed my name, took the sand out of my stomach, left triangles zigzagged across my waist.

A giant does not fit, because a giant is the sum of his parts: a body built large, lungs the size of palm leaves, enough room to carry something more than a bad back and a reason to turn the lights out.

Even now, I do not understand the size of things, how much space I take up in the world, how anyone can fit their body into such a small piece of fabric. I am reminded every day of how easily the body opens: how I catch my skin at the wrong angle with a fingernail, how if I press my thumb into my chest hard enough I can burst through. There is more to say here but I do not know if I have the room or if I have the patience to see how far skin can stretch. Here are things I do know: When skin is sliced open and bunched it dries to a white flake. The reason you cannot picture a giant on an airplane is because they burned his body. You and I will never be pharaohs because you must burn me too. Do not bury me in something larger than what I am.

Body Scissor

The secret is that I am tired of secrets.

A part of wrestling is the "rest hold"—a moment where both wrestlers are allowed to catch their breaths while still simulating action; it's a low-energy move where the wrestlers can use each other's body weight to regain their stamina. Kevin Owens calls himself the Master of the Chinlock to play up his heel persona; he knows how much the fans hate these moments of respite, so he applies them liberally in order to break the action for a moment and to let the boos rain down from the rafters.

The body scissor exists to let performers catch their breath: while on the ground, one wrestler wraps his legs around the other's waist. It is a move that does not seem to do anything—the wrestlers tilt their heads back as if there is a struggle we cannot possibly understand. It is the greatest trick in all of wrestling: a move that looks like it is cutting off oxygen but is, in fact, giving everyone a chance to breathe. It comes from a place of exhaustion, of wanting to carry around a little less weight, of wishing a tight tendon would just snap.

Here. Let us rest here for a moment.

A Giant Is Always Interrupting

Braun Strowman Is Never Finished

Because we prefer our giants to be finite, a man this large cannot evolve any further because he is at the end of what we perceive to be possible, what is plausible. His motions, too, are never finished. For all the talk of seasons and blowoffs, the story never truly ends: there is always a next town, another setup and breakdown, lines in electrical tape on the coliseum floor to show where the cameramen can bend down on one knee to make the world seem that much smaller. In the sense of forever, everything is minute. This is why it feels that time moves faster as we get older; we simply have more summers to compare to one another: the one where fire ants flooded my shoe, the one where the doors to the ambulance opened wide and they wheeled you in—I never thought the inside of anything man-made could be so bright. We are our own monsters, expecting anything in a life to make sense—as if there is a path that we can lay out in front of us in tape, in feet of cable. The characters we watch grow larger, yet younger, than us, until one day I will be among nothing but versions of myself. There are stories of lives flashing before people's eyes, of how they realize there was nothing to tell, of how they vow to do more with the time they have been given: They will go into the mountains. They will tell a stranger that they love them. My fear is that the story will go on forever— that I will live out everything that I ever did, that the flash will be a light that blinds me for a lifetime, then starts over again.

Topé con Hilo

The secret is most moves have two names.

The LeBell Lock is a crossface. Randy Orton's RKO is Diamond Dallas Page's Diamond Cutter is John Laurinaitis's Ace Crusher is a standing face cutter. The schoolboy looks like an O'Connor Roll, but it isn't. Every generic big-man bad guy has a sit-out powerbomb that he gives a new name to make it seem like he has a personality larger than his stature. It is a fallaway slam unless the wrestler is a Pacific Islander, then it is a Samoan drop. If the wrestler is fat, it is a bullfrog splash. You say *uranage* when you mean spike. A reverse piledriver is a tombstone. A reverse hurricanrana is poisoned. If you crash-land with your opponent, it's a Death Valley driver. I'm sorry that I keep bringing up death, but death is something that wrestling is known for: last men standing, and hell in a cell, and loser leaves town, sole survivors. The last move of the match is called a finisher for a reason: there is a definitive end. Someone has been finished, eradicated.

Any time a wrestler dives from inside the ring to the outside, it is called a suicide, as if they are taking their own life into their hands to end another's. Announcers shout out the suicide dive with reckless abandon, as if they have lived a life without loss. Occasionally, to make it sound more authentic, announcers adopt *lucha libre* terminology: the *topé suicida*—a suicide headbutt, as if translating the word removes it of its power, reminds people less of the time they received a phone call outside of a friend's home that said nothing but said everything. We can translate silence without needing to read the runes.

Sometimes they go a step further: a *topé con hilo*—translated to "threading headbutt," as if a body flies through the ropes as if it were a needle, as if this name wouldn't remind us of how tight a makeshift noose can be: a loop, a knot, and then through.

The wrestler hits the move—his opponent there to break his fall, before grabbing at his back, as if to say that he had risked everything to do what he had just done, that spinning through the air, if only for a moment, is something that should be impossible. That he had rebelled against gravity, or logic, or whatever needs defiance.

When a match is over, we focus only on the survivor; he is the only one left in the spotlight.

Another step further: *topé con hilo* is a mistranslation. Japanese wrestlers misinterpreted the phrase while watching *lucha libre* matches. Instead, the phrase is *topé con giro*, or "spinning headbutt"—we have lost rotation and gained a thread, a more direct way through. A needle eventually hits its mark or falls to the ground, whereas something else could simply spin forever, in constant rotation on the air as the rope twists and untwists until it is cut from the rafters. These days, we use the phrases interchangeably, as if language never mattered at all—anything to prevent us from saying the words that we should say, as if we have the one locution we cannot will ourselves to bring alive with our voice.

Vince McMahon and the Tending of the Flock

You, creator of worlds, destroyer of men. You, slick-haired, slick-tongued, with the slow rumble of a voice that has been layered with ash and pinecone, the bark of a tree cascading down your throat like it has been there all along—steadfast and rooted in cold ground since before any of us were a thought. We give you praise, we give you thanks, we give you a subtle roar when things go our way, a gentle bow of the head as we appreciate you for you instead of what you have become. You, false god. You, a man full of sweat and sand, you in a suit the color of a beautiful lake, you a color that you created.

You, one of us: you, the voice, you, in a cheap suit, zipped on, Velcroed in the back, you, interchangeable. You, knowing the names of all of the maneuvers as if you invented them: released hold, heel kick, brainbuster, backbreaker. You, crying after my heroes died. You, steadfast in your presentation. You, presenter of worlds.

Praise to you, hallelujah, praise for every red-chested slap, every unification, every beer-barrel-chested man I would never become, every long-haired snapback for emphasis, every fake punch meant to look beautiful. Every blonde with space tits, every Black man thuggish, every islander from the land of the rising sun. Every dead hero in the mold of a hero, every broken back and every brain busted.

I give myself unto you when my own father does not wish to answer questions, my mother secretly sliding tithes through cable wires to keep her child happy after skinny cruisers lifted his shirt up to expose the hairless fat beneath. The old television of my grandfather's brought home on a Sunday and hooked up by Monday is the first thing I could ever call my own: you among drawings of imaginary warriors pulled from magazines—fold-out posters where staple holes pierce stomachs that look nothing like mine.

When they ask if I am still loyal, Chairman, I am still loyal. I see your fiction in my dreams and wish to be a part of it: to pretend that this is all real and I am here among it, that I am beautiful and beloved, that I am a vampire, that I am from the future, that I am a turkey hatched from an egg. That you have changed my name, rearranged it so it is unrecognizable: when the crowds chant for me, they spit something new. Where too much of my name has been misspelled for too long, yours is the only true name left and it is that of your father. I am still loyal and I praise you with a knowing smile—I have not changed, because you have not changed. I know all of the tricks—the one with the slap to the thigh, the stomping of the mat, the chair always delivered to the broadest part of the body.

I close my eyes and I am created by you: I am picking up brutes over my shoulder, I am spinning them into oblivion. I send them crashing into crumpled heaps, I am hugging the breath out of strangers. I am wrapping my wrists. I am taping my ribs.

And yet there is no room for me here, where creativity can provide nothing other than a quick toss down a flight of stairs. You, god of something I hold dear, break me and make me whole again. Make me a businessman with a paisley tie. Make me disappear only to be reborn: a clown for the taking, a golem who eats his own fingers. Put me in a mask that keeps me from breathing.

LET ME TELL YOU SOMETHING

After the three count or the tap out, the referee
signals to the timekeeper to ring the bell, signifying
the end of the match. The story continues—the
victor wincing as the referee raises his arm to
demonstrate that he took damage during the match,
that no one leaves unscathed. Belts are raised high
above heads, turnbuckles are climbed. The loser
disappears from view, making sure that he remains
off-camera, hiding on the floor between the ring
and the audience barricade. When the time is right,
the loser will make his way back up the ramp to
the back. Sometimes we see him, depressed and
limping, as he disappears behind the curtain. Other
times, the lights go off in the arena, as if to say there
are some losses we are not meant to see.

Facewash

The secret is it's not as bad as it looks.

At some point most evenings, the conversation turns to scars. Whiskey has put us at our most vulnerable, so we show off the marks of our bodies—the tattoos that are only meant for lovers, the past traumas we can laugh about now because we lived through them. We talk about how the world took a part of us and how we wear the world on our skin. An improper intramural softball slide. An ill-fitting ankle brace. A glass table that cracked under the weight of a body. Chicken pox scabs worried with a fingernail.

In a sport where everything is meant to look real, despite knowing its inherent falsehoods, I am easily fooled. I think that every ankle is actually turned, that when a dive to the outside misses wildly, a shoulder has been separated. Perhaps this is because I expect the worst; as I've grown older, I find myself more cynical about bodies in general. How fragile mine can seem at a moment's notice. I think of all of the injuries I could never come back from: a broken femur, a shattered clavicle. I imagine that this gives me a high tolerance for pain—that if it isn't the worst thing imaginable, it isn't that bad. And yet it doesn't prevent me from thinking that my pancreas has stopped working because of a sharpness in my stomach after a long weekend away or that this tightness in my hamstring is a permanent condition, my tendons forever shortened to the point that I will never be able to walk in a straight line without curving inward.

The scars of wrestling are mostly internal—enlarged hearts, lesions on brain wrinkles. But those are never the marks that we remember. We think of Mick Foley's half ear. The chunk missing from the top of Seth Rollins's back tattoo. The permanent slice on William Regal's lip.

To control the narrative of our body, we start with the skin. I have no tattoos, but I have scars, the most prominent on the back of my hand, where my wrist buckled as I tried to catch a falling bronze statue—a story grander than what it left behind, as you can only see the hard tissue in the right light. Before I was torn open, I told a different story—of a small square dot on my ankle that I thought was caused by something in my youth. My story would change as I got older and more accustomed to lying about my body: a stray soccer cleat turned into a kick with some malice behind it—revenge for getting the best of my opponent on the field.

You can see the scars on Dusty Rhodes's forehead—how they look like a map of tributaries, of stories told and retold until they all blend together. They became more visible as he grew older, the wrinkles causing the scars to stick out a little farther than they once did, producing long lines where the skin lost its elasticity.

But to me, the thing I always remember about Dusty was a large discolored splotch on his stomach, right below his right pectoral muscle. Some matches it was redder than others, though it might've been how the arena light illuminates some things but not others. The stories range from an infection from a barbed wire match to the removal of the appendix. The most circulated tale is that it was a burn mark from a misfired fireball during a match in Japan in his youth. After

Dusty's passing, his son Cody talked about how Dusty was a larger-than-life figure and you could never tell if the stories about him were true or fiction: how he held the title of sky admiral or how he hid a donkey in his apartment. The truth about the splotch is that it was a birthmark—something that grew larger as he gained weight. It had just always been there.

I have an age spot on the side of my face, close to where my sideburn meets my hairline. It is off-color, a slightly raised bump that gets red every time I shave or when I am out in the sun for too long. These markings, they come from inside of us—in this case, an accumulation of too many aged skin cells until the spot protrudes from the skin. There are theories about how to prevent this from happening: spending less time in the sun or employing a rigorous skin-care routine. However, most doctors believe it to be inevitable—that this is something that happens with age, regardless of outside forces. The war of the body is always internal, our wounds hiding just below the skin, waiting for us to get our story straight.

Manami Toyota Wants to Return to a Body That Does Not Hurt Anywhere Anymore

Because we do not know if flowers feel pain, because we are not flowers. Mornings, I mask myself with the smell of orchids, of lemongrass, of black roses, because no part of what I am ever came from the earth. One day I hope to return—a wish to arrive somewhere I have never imagined. I live, here, smelling of oak moss, white truffle—anything but the scent of dirt.

ONE LAST THING

In Japanese wrestling, it is customary for fans to throw paper streamers in the ring to show their appreciation for their favorite wrestlers. The ring fills up with color quickly, often draping the wrestlers with long strands that stick to their skin. These displays are reserved for big occasions: title changes, returns of legends, or retirement matches. They represent the end of something that was supposed to end. What was meant to happen has happened.

My Mother Still Asks
about The Undertaker

In the same way that she asks about my friends from college,
though she forgets the names more often than not: the one
who left the country never to return, the one who left the
country and came back, the one who never left, the one who
never left but left you. I tell her everyone is doing fine—I
have seen photographs of children, pictures of backyards, of
homemade wind chimes. Some of them are dead—not in the
way that The Undertaker is dead or is not dead but gone the
same way I answer "Whatever happened to?" questions when
I reveal I spent most Monday nights watching the Deadman
keep his balance on a tightrope or set another casket on fire
instead of spending two more hours with someone who
would be gone one day.

I can't begin to tell you why I am still here and they are
not, why someone my mother asked about would ask about
me—whether I had kept the weight off, whether I had left the
valley of the shadow of death that I must wander by choice,
whether anyone had ever loved me the way an open palm
loves lightning.

The Deadman is still here too—in the same way that so
many more are not, those who did not dare tempt fate by

claiming to be the bringer of death, as death loves a good joke more than a blanched skull. In this world, if you say his name enough he will appear—he will turn the lights out, he will set where you stand on fire.

And yet he only appears when summoned, the same way we chant the names of ghosts in mirrors, the same way we hear a word for the first time and then cannot stop hearing it in whispers and on billboards. This is because you and I wish to make patterns out of everything: for every hero, a villain, for every undead creature, a brother of fire.

No one believes in spells anymore, but they believe in fear, in how we claim to be our own witchcraft: we can say the right words in the right order and unlock what we once were and what we hope to be. It is a beautiful thing to be thought of this way: we can simply speak something into the world enough times and have it return to us, like holding on to a small smooth stone and saying your name to bring you back from wherever it is you have been hiding.

I believe that one day I will be missed, and you will say the right things, and I will come back like a bell's echo off of an empty apartment building. I will come back like nothing you've ever seen before but everything you remember: my hair will be a little shorter, my eyes a bit more weathered. This is the only way you'll be able to tell I have been gone. We have all pretended to be dead at some point, as if we can conjure up what it is to no longer be here without waiting to make our immaculate return, all smoke and mirrors before bursting through the curtain. We close our eyes. We pretend that we are sleeping. We don't move when our names are called.

Whatever happened to me, they'll say—yet I will not be around to hear it. You'll hear I went up into the mountains, never to return. You'll hear I died in a desert. A grand explosion. A lake of fire—my toes too close to the edge as I dissolve into vapor. How we condense in the sky. How we rise.

This, too, is myth. If we believe in patterns, in how we feel a radiating heat on the side of our face every time we think you are here, or in blue cars, or in the sameness of every match—the stare down, the palm strike—we cannot believe in coincidence. We cannot believe in constantly looking for something majestic, in soil burning, in how I just saw you, in how I was thinking about reaching out to tell you about my day right before I heard that you were gone, here and then not. Instead, let me ask new questions—let me answer queries about what is left, whether I have heard anything, whether I have seen anything. It is summer now. This morning it was too hot to run. They are paving the sidewalk across the street from where you used to live—they are repairing the lines underground. I saw someone who looked like you while I was stopped at an intersection. I'll believe in anything that brings you back.

On Dressing Up as Goldust
for Halloween

He applies the makeup himself: a video of him drawing the outlines of where the black foundation shall go shows the long sweeps he makes—up and over the contours of his cheekbones, over the tops of tightly shut eyelids. The patterns have gotten more elaborate as he has gotten older: earlier days included a squirt of gold face paint into cracked palms, a wash of sparkle over splotched skin chafed red from too many drinks or too many headlocks. Now, there are angles that you've never seen: the flaring of nostrils, the erasing of eyebrows, the caking of the neck until beard stubble cannot push through the gold like an unwanted dandelion.

I cannot do this on my own. My hands do not turn the right way: they grow tired from their own mechanics; they cannot hold anything worth holding. Every finger I have is broken except for the thumbs, only spared by my clumsiness: a misjudged football, a slip on the ice braced for every way but the correct one.

As you sit on the coffee table in a blond wig, you paint circles around my eyes. We start with the gold first, my head shaved for the artifice: the makeup is soaked up by the dryness in my cheeks. You are concerned that this will be inauthentic: that the colors will smudge together and there will be no way to tell the difference between the gold and the black, that they will combine into a sparkly mud of nothing— bronze instead of gold, a dullness less bizarre, a second loser instead of something victorious.

The man beneath the makeup spoke only in quotes from famous starlets and dashing leads, about always being ready for one's close-up. You are the only one I allow to look me in the eye—the rest of the time I keep my nose to the ground or I look toward the sky as if I have forgotten everything I've ever wanted to say and am active in the mystique of re-membering. As if all I can remember is my name and even then I am uncertain about how it sprawls from underneath my tongue—as if I used to speak with perfect diction, never stutter or stumble or fear that a syllable would get caught and echo back down my throat and into my lungs. I, too, speak in quotations: things I have said before, forgetting to tell you about fears, about deaths and marriages. Instead, I tell you about my day over and over again—about things I once said, about overheard nothings, about things you have told me that I have already told.

You know nothing about wrestling—about how men much larger than me fly through the air, how it is all choreo-graphed, how no one actually gets hurt—but you know about how everything hurts. You ask me who I am being, again— gold paint and leotard, someone so grandiose yet so inconse-quential. We are playing pretend; we are make-believing. You ask who you are supposed to be: the lovely accompaniment, the director, the producer, the woman in lamé, the name you forget because it means nothing, another character, a small bit role in a story that has no end—a constant revolution of characters coming and going, losing one's way, giving up the gold ghost, acknowledging that all of this is false. We all know how the story ends: in redemption, in putting the makeup back on, in slithering over feathers, in remembering that some things are worth remembering and others are worth repeating.

You go back over the parts of my face that wish to remain uncovered—the dark concealer fading as it absorbs into my skin, as if I am trying to fight the cover-up. I tell you to mind my lips, to make sure my jaw is covered, that I look as real as possible. We buy a cigar from the corner store to complete your outfit. You buy a dress that you will never wear again. You do this because you know this is important to me: to be mistaken for someone who wakes up in hotel rooms states away, who has brothers, daughters, who pretends to be hurt when he is not hurt. We will play the parts that neither of us were born to play. We will never break character: we will pose with strangers; we will drink gin through straws so we do not ruin the lipstick. We will return home, smoky and exhausted, a black smudge on your cheek. You will help me wash the paint off from behind my ears—I will spit black and gold when your head is turned. We will go to bed with our hair wet. We will wake up the next morning, and the next morning, and the next morning. I will remember your name each and every time. I will not forget my lines.

Mankind's Entrance Music Is Different Than His Exit Music

Upon arrival, strings. A brooding—a clutching at one's chest as if to protect one's body as if it is a bird that needs warmth, as if catgut and trill can somehow make us feel whole again. Everyone gets their music played—the goal is to get it played twice, to have your hand raised as you paw at your chin with your wrist to show that while you secured the pin, you took a few good shots along the way.

In the backseats of cars, we talk about what our songs would be—the melodies that would play as we made our way down the ramp toward an inevitable victory, as we slid underneath the bottom rope and scaled the turnbuckle to let the fans know that we are here for a fight. We choose crunching guitars, because we are boys—we are desperately searching for something louder than we are. We queue up songs as we descend staircases into basements, embankments off of back porches. We pose. The tapes pop. The discs skip. The timing is never right.

I have spent my entire life perfecting my entrance.

But the bell rings and the music fades out, and I am alone in my body with my fists up. The chords have left me. I should have never come here. I should have never pretended that I was something that I am not. If you learn how to fight by watching others pretend to fight, you'll be left with a bleeding ear and a missing tooth—begging that the suffering, for once, be on the other side. Give me my beating— let the crowd that gathered think I am having the time of my goddamn life. My black eye, my cut tongue. My body as hollow as a violin. The soul post broken in two, a whole step behind. Play my music, one last time. Let someone else interrupt—the sound of shattering glass, a drum fill, anything to drown out the muffled sound of having a hole stomped through. The songs I used to sing will never save me.

Instead, let me hear my exit music, just once—the fade to black and the rolling of credits, my name appearing in white. I have imagined the beginning and I have imagined the end: exhausted, lying in the middle of the ring while the piano plays. The day is nice, the air cold, the sun warm. Tonight, let me be the man I almost was.

Lie here with me for a moment. Look: the confetti is streaming in from behind every barricade—long wisps of papier-mâché and ticker tape bouncing across the mat, the falling colors sticking to my sweat-slicked shoulders. Let everyone clap until their arms grow tired and their palms turn pink. Watch them file out of their seats and into their cars. Think of how they are too excited to sleep because they can't wait to tell everyone the next day that they were there; they saw the impossible. No one will believe them, but they were there—they saw it with their own eyes. They saw what was meant to be seen. It's time for you to go home too. Leave me here. I'll be here in the empty arena, buried in every color you can imagine. Leave the light on. Lock the doors and leave. Let the music keep playing. Tonight, let me pretend that I am victorious. Tonight, let me find my own way back.

CHAMPIONSHIP CELEBRATION

Thank you to the kind folks at the University of North Carolina Press, especially Lucas Church, for taking this book from the midcard to the main event. I am forever in debt to y'all and will root for the Tar Heels in sporting events against the Blue Devils from this point forward. You have it in writing.

Love and thanks to my fellow writers who also happen to be wrestling fans: Elle Collins, Mike Chin, Ryan Satin, David Dennis Jr., and Andrew Cartwright. The superkick will never be lowbrow.

A very special thanks to Colette Arrand and Todd Kaneko, direct inspirations in writing and finishing this book. I'm sorry I didn't write a Batista essay.

Another very special thanks to Sal Pane and Theresa Beckhusen, hype folks to the stars. I'm so grateful to have y'all in my corner.

Thank you to anyone I've ever watched a PPV with and chipped in for pizza, namely David A. Smith, Trey Irby, Rob Cramer, Will Nevin, Kate Furek, Daniel Di Bona, Kenon A. Brown, Jeff Hanson, and Blaine Duncan.

Thank you to all of my friends who have kindly nodded

along as I explained to them the nuances of a triple-threat match, namely Steve Kowalski, Ashley Sheehan, Chris Mink, Jenifer Park, Alon Wingard, Abbas Abidi, P. J. Williams, Connor Towne O'Neill, Shaelyn Smith, Ryan Bollenbach, Austin Stickney, Joe Lucido, Kayleb Candrilli, Farren Stanley, Jeremy Hawkins, Matt Parolie, Rebecca Birmingham, Michael Martone, Patti White, Austin Whitver, James Eubanks, Jessica Johnson, Brandi Wells, Bob Weatherly, Andy Johnson, Juan Carlos Reyes, Robyn Hammontree, John Hammontree, Katie Jean Shinkle, Susan Doss, Bo Hicks, Lauren Gail, Riley Bingham, Mike Fitzgerald, Kori Hensell, Cat Leeches, Sara Beth Riddle, Wells Addington, Colin Rafferty, Elizabeth Wade, Natalie Lima, Matt Minicucci, Darren Demaree, B. J. Hollars, Daniel Wagner, Natalie Wagner, Tessa Carter, Daniel Bernal, Joe Loye, and so many others. I can't wait to celebrate this victory and many others with y'all.

Thanks to my Armed Mind family, especially Mike Rudin, Jackie Ling, Dan Martin, Chris Lee, Michael Mitchell, and Milena Westarb. Thanks for putting up with me suggesting wrestling partners on every ideation.

There's a quote in wrestling and in writing about how in the business there are a lot of acquaintances but few friends. Thankfully, I've never found that to be true. Love and gratitude to Aubrey Hirsch, Matt Bell, R. A. Villanueva, Kaveh Akbar, Ira Sukrungruang, Mark Cugini, Ashley C. Ford, Karissa Chen, Jill Talbot, Noah Cho, Siân Griffiths, Aaron Burch, Chris Gonzalez, Bruce Owens Grimm, Moira McAvoy, Sejal Shah, Roxane Gay, Lyz Lenz, Kendra Fortmeyer, Alissa Nutting, Dean Bakopoulos, Sarah Rose Etter, Erin Slaughter, Brad Efford, Lauren Cross, Kelly Davio, Blake Butler, Elizabeth Morris Lakes, Lauren Milici, Caroline Crew, Leila Chatti, Adrienne Celt, Amorak Huey, Jared Yates Sexton, Ander Monson, Silas Hansen, and so many more that

I know I am missing. Thank you for making writing a lot less lonely.

Thank you to all of my students: you're the reason I keep fighting.

Thank you to Daniel Bryan, Io Shirai, and Minoru Suzuki for helping me explain to people why I love this thing I love.

To Jason McCall and Camellia Grass: y'all know.

Thanks to Summer The Greyhound who let me use her office while I finished edits on this book.

To Mom and Dad, sorry my love of wrestling wasn't just a phase. Thank you for buying the Royal Rumble every year. Thank you for loving me unconditionally.

Thank you to Tasha for putting up with me and all of my obsessions. I love you more than wrestling.

And finally, thank you for reading. May your life be five stars.

CREDITS

"Mark Henry, the World's Strongest Man, Is the World's Strongest Man" originally published in *Monkeybicycle*.

"Triple H and Why There Are Fights in Locker Rooms" originally published in *Matchbook*.

"Heartbreak, or How I Felt When Shawn Michaels Threw His Best Friend through a Window" originally published in *Banango Lit*.

"A Giant is Always Interrupting: Jorge The Giant" originally published in *Newfound*.

"Hulk Hogan Comes to Tuscaloosa" originally published in *Black Sun Lit*.

"Ric Flair Has More Cars Than You Have Friends" originally published in *The Pinch*.

"The Ultimate Warrior Believes in Nothing but Forever" originally published in *Bending Genre*.

"Bret Hart and the Finished Dungeons of Our Youth" originally published in *Rappahannock Review*.

"Yokozuna and the Calling of Names That Aren't Our Own" originally published in *Booth*.

"Owen Hart and the Finite Life of Ropes" originally published in *The Economy*.

"Everyone Has a 'Macho Man' Randy Savage Impersonation" originally published in *Fanzine*.

"The wwe Hall of Fame Does Not Exist: An Inauguration Poem" originally published in *The Rumpus*.

"There Will Be No Mention of _____'s Name Tonight" originally published in *Fanzine*.

"John Cena Is the Only Thing That Is Left Here" originally published in *Cartridge Lit*.

"'Stone Cold' Steve Austin Cannot Be Forgotten" originally published in *Phoebe*.

"Brock Lesnar and the Woman I Am About to Marry Are Both Billed from Minneapolis–St. Paul, Minnesota" originally published in *The Collagist*.

"Mr. Perfect Alone in a Room Where He Will Die" originally published in *Big Lucks*.

"Chris Jericho and How The World Ends" originally published in *TriQuarterly*.

"A Giant Is Always Interrupting: Paul, the Apostle, the Giant" originally published in *The Hunger*.

"On Razor Ramon Entering the Ring for the First Time and the Last Time" originally published in *Mojo*.

"The Rock Covered Up His Brahma Bull Tattoo the Same Weekend I Watched Him in the Film *San Andreas*" originally published in *New Limestone Review*.

"A Giant Is Always Interrupting: The Eighth Wonder of the World Visits the First Wonder of the World" originally published in *NANO Fiction*.

"Vince McMahon and the Tending of the Flock" originally published in *storySouth*.

"On Dressing Up as Goldust for Halloween" originally published in *Cease, Cows*.